BEING CALLED, BEING GAY

BEING CALLED, BEING GAY

...

Discernment for Ministry
in the Episcopal Church

Gregory L. Millikin

FOREWORD BY MARY D. GLASSPOOL

CHURCH
PUBLISHING
INCORPORATED

Copyright © 2018 by Gregory L. Millikin

All rights reserved. No part of this book may be reproduced, stored in a retrieval system, or transmitted in any form or by any means, electronic or mechanical, including photocopying, recording, or otherwise, without the written permission of the publisher.

Unless otherwise noted, the Scripture quotations contained herein are from the New Revised Standard Version Bible, copyright © 1989 by the Division of Christian Education of the National Council of Churches of Christ in the U.S.A. Used by permission. All rights reserved.

Church Publishing
19 East 34th Street
New York, NY 10016
www.churchpublishing.org

Cover design by Marc Whitaker, MTWdesign
Layout and typesetting by Beth Oberholtzer

Library of Congress Cataloging-in-Publication Data

Names: Millikin, Gregory, author.
Title: Being called, being gay : discernment for ministry in the Episcopal Church / Gregory Millikin ; foreword by Mary Glasspool.
Description: New York, NY : Church Publishing, [2018] | Includes bibliographical references.
Identifiers: LCCN 2018022110 (print) | LCCN 2018034457 (ebook) | ISBN 9781640650138 (ebook) | ISBN 9781640650121 (pbk.)
Subjects: LCSH: Episcopal Church—Clergy—Appointment, call, and election. | Gay clergy—United States. | Ordination—Episcopal Church. | Homosexuality--Religious aspects—Episcopal Church.
Classification: LCC BX5965 (ebook) | LCC BX5965 .M55 2018 (print) | DDC 262/.1437308664—dc23
LC record available at https://lccn.loc.gov/2018022110

CONTENTS

Foreword by Mary D. Glasspool — vii
Author's Note — x
Introduction — xiii

Chapter 1: Awakening — 1

Chapter 2: The Historic Moment — 19

Chapter 3: The Process — 35

Chapter 4: Living with Authenticity — 53

Chapter 5: Priesthood and Sexual Identity — 73

Chapter 6: No and Not Yet — 87

Chapter 7: Yes — 101

Conclusion — 113
For Further Reading — 119
Acknowledgments — 121

FOREWORD

Greg Millikin has written a much-needed book for our world today. Not only does the church need to hear and really *listen to* voices that have previously been institutionally excluded from a conversation about appropriate leadership, so also does the larger society. In part, Greg has offered his voice to articulate what it's like for a person who identifies as a member of what Greg terms the LGBT+ community to engage the process of discernment for ordained ministry in the Episcopal Church. Greg does this using three fundamental building blocks.

First, he tells his own story. Marked by honesty, thoughtfulness, and humor, Greg shares with us moments of doubt, "light bulb" incidents when life took on new clarity through the advice or counsel of a friend or mentor, and the affirmations that over the long haul led to his ordinations to the diaconate and the priesthood. Supplementing his own story, Greg explores topics that have a particular bearing on LGBT+ people: *shame, integrity,* and *authenticity* among them. While having been sponsored by a diocese that is known to be progressive and supportive of the LGBT+ community (Los Angeles), Greg writes with awareness of the plights of others in different dioceses and parts of the country.

Second, Greg sets his story in the historical context of the church's story of wrestling with sexuality as well as spirituality. Chapter two of the book deals explicitly with events

FOREWORD

that helped to shape the current time in which we now live: Stonewall, Alfred Kinsey, the ordination of women in the Episcopal Church, and the consecration of Gene Robinson as the first openly gay bishop in the Anglican Communion are all part of this story. Each of us has a larger context to our lives, which informs and influences the choices we make and the lives we live. Greg offers the larger context within which his own discernment took place, and this is not only helpful, but also essential.

Third, Greg engages holy scripture, tradition, and reason as the foundation of his book. Each chapter begins with a quote from scripture, and very often quotes from poets, writers, musicians, and other scholars. I rejoice in this engagement because of the overriding occupational hazard of isolation for ordained ministers regardless of their sexuality! Greg models for us throughout his book a reaching out to scripture, to mentors and friends, to history and heritage, so that the conversation is a *dialogue* with many participants, not a *monologue*.

After I read Greg's manuscript for the first time, I found myself challenged to reflect on my own call to ordained ministry, including the similarities and differences with how Greg has written about his call. It was during my college years (1972–1976) that I began to discern a vocation to ordained ministry and concomitantly began to discover my sexuality. Both these areas were sources of intense struggle for me, as I wrestled with such questions as *Did God hate me (since I was a homosexual)?* or *Did God love me? Did I hate (or love) myself? Was it really possible, not to mention appropriate, for women to be priests?* My father was an Episcopal priest, and his answer to this last question was a resounding **NO**. True to his own colors he never publicly supported women's ordination, although I became something of an exception to the rule.

God was still transcendent and other to me as I entered Episcopal Divinity School in the fall of 1976, just as the

FOREWORD

General Convention in Minneapolis was wrestling to recognize the reality of women called to be priests, the new prayer book, and what to do with the Philadelphia Eleven and the Washington Five as we termed them at EDS. My role models at that time represented two different ways of doing things in response to God's call: Carter Heyward—one of the Philadelphia Eleven and a professor at my seminary—and Carol Anderson, a deacon who made the decision to wait for the church to "make up its mind" before offering herself to the priesthood. Carter, for me, represented the courage to break through barriers—not without cost—in order to become fully the person God is calling you to become. Carol represented the sacrificial love of the Church that manifested itself in restraint, and also came at great cost. Both of these courageous women have continued to model for me the integrity of responding to God's call with your whole person, being exactly who you are.

As I look back, the Episcopal Church has come a long way in a relatively brief period of history. And yet we continue to struggle—wrestle may be a better word—reminding us of Jacob wrestling with the angel, as we discern as a church what God may be calling us to now.

In summing up the need for a spiritual director, Greg writes this: "Adrift seemingly with no bearings even if the path is being distilled to something attainable, it is easy to feel isolated as a queer postulant. But you will never be alone." I'm thankful for Greg, his story, his willingness to write it, and the concomitant challenge to reflect on our own stories. My hope and my prayer is that just as I have been challenged by Greg's book, you, the reader, will be challenged, sustained, and inspired by his words as well.

The Rt. Rev. Mary D. Glasspool,
Bishop Assistant, the Episcopal Diocese of New York
April 30, 2018

AUTHOR'S NOTE

The ever-shifting sands of sociopolitical correctness make for a challenge in committing to labels in a published work. So, until we reach a second edition (God willing), I am choosing decisively to use the label "LGBT+" in this book.

As soon as I write it, and as soon as someone reads it, there will be objections. Where is the Q? Where's the I? Why the +? Why not just "gay and lesbian"? How did you get a book deal?

I suppose the most pertinent question you may be asking is, Why bother confining people to labels? Well, we are human beings. And in a book that deals heavily with theology about the expansive cosmic love of God, we must confess that we will always come up short. In my human fallacy, I tend to believe we have covered a majority of the bases with the term LGBT, sans +. It took me a long time to switch from "gay" to then "gay and lesbian" to then a four-letter acronym, GLBT. I remember around 2009 or so, I consciously tried to train my brain to make my mouth say "*L*"-GBT, the more popular formula now.

As of this writing, I am concerned that going beyond the four letters in the acronym risks distracting a reader, raises too many tangential questions, and in many cases adds fur-

AUTHOR'S NOTE

ther complication. *I* refers to intersex, a name for someone who is unable to accept one gender over the other, or perhaps is refraining from such a decision. *Q* at first seems like it might stand for "queer" which actually would be redundant in my view; anyone who is not straight is queer, in one sense. Queer has been used pejoratively as an epithet for the gay community, but it has had something of a renaissance in recent years—reclaimed from within the community by those who were inhibited by its use originally. In fact, the essential brand of theology from the perspective, or through the lens, of homosexuality is known in the last forty years in academic circles as *queer theology* (we delve into detail on this topic in chapter 5). But no, *Q* usually means "questioning." Now, I certainly worry as a priest and as a queer man for anyone who is struggling with his or her sexuality. But for terms of labeling (which, again, is something to which many readers are *already* allergic) someone who is questioning, in my eyes, has basically let the genie out of the bottle already.

So, when I need to employ an acronym, I have settled on the increasingly popular +. It means, effectively, LGBT *plus* any other label for which time, space, and imagination simply cannot allow. You will see, from here on out, either the description "queer" or the acronym *LGBT+* referring to our lesbian sisters, gay brothers, bisexual friends, and transgender persons (those who have transitioned at least emotionally and mentally, if not physically, from male to female or from female to male). At the very least, I hope you will allow me some grace in this decision. We cannot all be happy, but we can appreciate that someone has agonized over something like this. You will find I may use *LBGT+* and *queer* interchangeably throughout this book.

And for the subset who thinks labels are detrimental? I actually tend to agree; I wish we did not need labels. Yet

AUTHOR'S NOTE

ever since cavemen and women looked to the sky and gave a name to their creator, we have been a human race obsessed with taxonomies.

And, for that matter, God.
And, sex.
But mostly God.

INTRODUCTION

Before I formed you in the womb I knew you, and before you were born I consecrated you. (Jer. 1:5)

This above all: to thine own self be true.
—*Hamlet,* Act I, Scene III

In the summer of 2001, at the age of twenty-two, I came out to myself. Coming out to my family and friends took several more years. Later, in the winter of 2009, I came out as called to ordained ministry. Now I use the term "coming out" for the latter event because, in the years since, it is the best phrase I can find to describe the process. In order to be fully aware of my spiritual self, I had to be honest about my physiological self. I had to be aware of my own sexual identity.

Therein lies the quandary—and the delight—in this book, which seeks to explore the challenge and grace of being both a member of the LGBT+ community and a leader in the Episcopal Church. Research and analysis of the last several years of the life of this Christian family, laid out in these pages, will illustrate what my instincts proved true: that the search for one's place in God's kingdom has a great deal to do with one's search for sexual truth.

Recent history of the Episcopal Church and human sexuality have already shown that the intersection of these topics can be volatile. Christendom has long had a complicated

INTRODUCTION

relationship with sexuality and sexual expression. With the exception of the ordination of women, which began in 1974 in the Episcopal Church, perhaps no other topic related to gender or sexual identity has garnered more rumination—or debate—than homosexuality. The case for or against the inclusion of LGBT+ women and men in our sanctuaries was the first great battle in recent decades; lately marriage equality has been the hot topic. However, the role of gay men and women as ordained leaders in our churches has always seemed to lurk in the background as a major complicating factor in the image of the body of Christ.

It nearly goes without saying at this stage that the ordination of the Rt. Rev. V. Gene Robinson to the episcopate in 2003 marked the most significant turning point for the Episcopal Church on this matter. And while this triggered a schism in the United States as well as ripple effects in the Anglican Communion worldwide, I hope to use this book to show a perspective often neglected in the media and church politicking. I offer one tangible, personal example: when Robinson was consecrated bishop, I had just decided to permanently ignore the persistent inclination to explore a possibility of becoming an Episcopal priest. The reason? I had just come out; openly gay people could not be priests. The consecration of Gene Robinson changed everything for me and for countless others. Suddenly, the rules of the game had changed, and it seemed for a moment in time that the sky was the limit as to where one may follow his or her calling.

Now we have entered into a new chapter in American society and, indeed, in the Episcopal Church. Same-sex marriage is legal in this country as a result of the 5-4 ruling of the Supreme Court of the United States in *Obergefell v. Hodges* in June of 2015. As of the Episcopal Church's General Convention in July 2018, same-sex marriage is now available to all couples who seek the sacrament in

America. Furthermore, the influx of LGBT+ women and men into seminaries and training for leadership in the Episcopal Church in the last decade is now in line with a denomination like the United Church of Christ (long the front-runner in this respect). Being queer and being a priest is now an option—and a viable one, at that. This is remarkable when one considers that an openness in this manner about sexual identity could have been a cause for disqualification only a dozen or so years ago.

So what can gay men and women do with these two callings, these two "coming out" stories? How are they transposed? How are they interposed?

This book follows a tradition started in modern classics of the faith, which for decades were the standard-bearers for persons beginning a discernment process to the diaconate or the presbyterate in the Episcopal Church. Until recently, *the* handbook for aspirants beginning to walk this journey was *Listening Hearts: Discerning a Call in Community*. One need only mention a feeling of being pulled toward leadership in the Church, and a priest would almost instinctually chuck a beat-up copy of *Listening Hearts* into his or her hands. This and other works by authors like Parker Palmer challenged the reader to develop a practice of listening to God's will and purpose through prayer and practice. But what if there was a new handbook aimed specifically at those beginning to discern the right use of their talents—those who were of the LGBT+ community?

Therefore, we begin to look at God's call through this lens of homosexuality. If we are made in the image of God, the *imago dei*, which this book presumes, then any deep exploration of our faith is contingent on a mature understanding of our sexuality and all it entails (no matter where one falls on the spectrum between straight and gay). This journey of call begins in earnest with chapter one's subject: integrity. Shakespeare got it right. The need to be honest with oneself is paramount, and it is linked with the need for all people to be honest with God. We are meant to always ask ourselves, "What is it exactly that God wants me to do?" This is a question that begins as soon as the mind is ready to deal with it, sometime around puberty, if not sooner. It is no coincidence that one's sexual identity begins to rise to the surface at about that time as well. God has ideas for each of us, and it is not reserved for deacons, priests, and bishops. Each of us is called by God. In the church, lay members are worship leaders, vestry members, choirmasters, senior wardens and junior wardens, treasurers; they run the bookstores, they lead the alto section in the choir, and they teach classes. Beyond our churches, members are leaders in countless fields from law to medicine to industry, in their homes and their communities. In each of these realms, clergy and laity may discern how God may be calling them to serve and to lead. The ultimate point, as Barbara Cawthorne Crafton succinctly puts it, is that "each of us is called to something."[1] Discovering which of these roles is the right path, in the church or outside the church, makes up the work of discernment. And the Episcopal Church has formalized a timeless practice of how leaders are lifted up from their own community.

Next, there is the notion of recognizing the historical moment in which LGBT+ people find themselves. Put simply, what do queer people bring to the Church? What talents or gifts can a gay man bring to preaching on the Old Testament? What might a transgender leader offer to social justice ministries? The LGBT+ minority enters a new age when its particular gifts influence monumental change in the Church.

Once a person begins the process of discernment in a parish or comparable faith community, any number of formalities come into play. For a queer person beginning this inward and outward journey in community, it can be an anxious time. Chapter three explains the general process of discernment, highlighting the important steps and potential pitfalls along the way for queer seekers.

The fourth chapter explores the authentic lifestyle. Now this is not to be confused with *lifestyle choice*; "lifestyle choice" used to be the standard term for insinuating that a homosexual was somehow choosing this identity, as if biology played no part in the sexual identity. Science has become a partner with faith and society in this arena. Because sexual identity has been proven to be biological, discussion now turns to lifestyle as *example*. In other words, how does a holy queer person live his or her life? And can his or her authenticity, behavior, disposition, sense of humor, or generosity become an example for others?

The discernment process tries to identify a person's predilection to the gifts of ordained ministry one way or another. Once the LGBT+ person is on the path to the priesthood (to focus on one role), the questions of sexuality become heightened because the stakes become higher. A priest is set apart to lead communities pastorally and sacramentally. A priest therefore ought not to be defined by his or her sexuality; at the same time, a priest should not neglect sexual identity. Indeed, sexuality is a theological issue. This fifth chapter, then, examines these poles, drawing on the work of queer theology. The argument will be made that we need a via media here.

The sixth chapter examines rejection. Any book about discernment in the Church must prepare the reader for the strong possibility that his or her sense of a calling—especially if that sense is specific—may be usurped. God could have other plans for you. The community could have other plans for you. And, yes, the community could fail you (the Church, after all, is a human endeavor). How we deal with rejection is really a question of how we deal with life. For an LGBT+ person, the assumption that homophobia may

INTRODUCTION

have played a part in the *No* answer is a given. Parsing out whether this rejection is the work of fallible humans or whether this is the work of the Holy Spirit somehow is the subject of this chapter.

On the flip side, as the final chapter examines, acceptance for some can be just as scary. What happens when your sense of calling has been affirmed by your faith community? What happens next? And what other challenges will come your way now that you are lifted up by the people to be a leader in Christ's Church (and not just any leader, but a *queer* one)? As the book draws to a close, the study turns to the next phase of discernment: the *Yes* answer.

Much of the "work" of *Being Called, Being Gay* is to serve as a guide for LGBT+ persons curious about their particular experience of being called as one out of many to serve in the Episcopal Church. In that respect, this is a guidebook for the road ahead for that person. I attempted to leaven each chapter with three ingredients: description of the discernment process and polity of the Episcopal Church; context in the sociopolitical history of the LGBT+ movement; and, hopefully with some lightheartedness, personal anecdotal evidence. If there is one thing I have learned so far in life, it is that discernment and human sexuality are always best examined in terms of faith, history, and personal emotion. For a student of modern Christianity, a student of any age, this writing may also be useful in studying how Christianity responds to and is in conversation with human sexuality. On a broader level, this is for the parishioner or worshiper who may have a new priest who is gay, lesbian, bisexual, or transgender. Hopefully this book colors in the background for that person in the pew, helping to illustrate the comingling of spirituality and sexuality. And maybe, just maybe, it can serve to illuminate those who are not yet comfortable with the queer priest.

If it does anything right, it will affirm that God meant for there to be queer leaders in the Church.

This is also a very personal book. It is uniquely my own story, concerning events in my discernment that one may find valuable for their own story (or, conversely, not at all helpful).

To that end, I did indeed begin this book by coming out to the reader. In my view, Jeremiah reported the truth: at the end of the day, God knew us before we were even formed in the womb. Any other exercise of trying to be someone you are not—to your own self—is a fool's errand. In this respect, I also show my cards. The mystery of where I fall on the sexuality debate is thus removed; I am clearly in support of full and equal inclusion of LGBT+ women and men in society and in the Church. That includes ordained leadership. But any baptized Christian (and most certainly an Episcopal priest) is expected to uphold a baptismal vow to seek and serve Christ in *all* persons. Entering into conversation with those who do not agree with us is the greatest challenge of our faith. It is also the most important thing we as Christians can do while we live out our lives together on this Earth. In that spirit, I welcome the reader who is still uncomfortable with the "other," particularly the LGBT+ other. With any luck, we can teach one another a thing or two.

But make no mistake, it is now normal to have queer leaders in the Church. The dust from Gene Robinson's consecration, the creation of ACNA[2] and the breakaway churches, the protests and the objections have mostly faded into the past. Now churches and faith communities are learning to live with queer clergy and lay leaders as they were in the 1970s when female priests first stepped up to altars across the United States in droves. Furthermore, in the wake of powerful social justice movements of recent years, from Black Lives Matter to the sexual harassment allegations of 2017 and the dawning of the #metoo movement, the time has come for the marginalized to claim authority and equality. In the shadow of these events, the queer community is finding its voice in leadership both inside and outside of the church walls. Queer persons of faith process their vocation, or their sense of calling, like any other would: trying desperately to listen to God speaking through prayer and through the words and actions of others. This is the essential work of discernment, and this is where we begin our journey.

Notes

1. Barbara Cawthorne Crafton, *Called* (New York: Church Publishing, 2017), ix.

2. The Anglican Communion in North America is one of the significant branches of formerly Episcopalian churches and leaders who left or "broke away" from the Episcopal Church in the years since Robinson's consecration.

1
Awakening

"Here I am." (Exod. 3:4)

On Mount Sinai, Moses, the eighty-year-old shepherd toiling with his flock, finds a burning bush. Moses approaches the bush, and the voice of God calls out to get his attention: "Moses! Moses!" Moses responds with the Hebrew word *hineni*, or in English, "Here I am."

So begins the journey of Moses, a call narrative in and of itself that indeed began many years before when the infant child was placed in the basket down the Nile. But now at this ripe age in Exodus 3, Moses is drawn into dialogue with God about his vocation. And Moses, in all his Mosesness, will struggle, debate, question, and wrestle with this calling. But he will do so with a great degree of honesty—with himself, and with the Lord God.

• • •

Honesty might be the most important word in this book about sexuality and call. It is the word that marks the intersection between the two topics, the intersection I am keen to inspect in these pages. In fact, in all honesty, the journey of discovery with respect to one's sexual identity runs parallel to that same person's call to serve God in any capacity. They are both journeys of discovery, and they are both marked by a great need to be honest with oneself.

To begin, it may be helpful to examine these two parallel tracks one by one. Let us start with the honesty needed in the realm of sexuality. The general assumption about human sexuality is that we, female and male humans, usually start figuring out our sexuality at puberty (typically ten to thirteen for girls, twelve to fifteen for boys). That may in fact be true; but the reality is that many children, encouraged by their increasingly culture-savvy parents, start to explore their gender and sexual identities at incredibly young ages. It is now believed that children begin to be aware of gender identification somewhere between two-and-a-half and four years old.[1] I know of at least two families in my life in the last ten years who have processed the unexpected awakening that their toddler-aged son is choosing to wear dresses. In an age of *Frozen*, there are some little boys who feel they can best express themselves (at an age where expressiveness is pretty difficult) by dressing like Princess Elsa.

Will these two boys grow up to be gay or bisexual men? Are they on a path toward transitioning to women? The answer is of course joyously unclear. This is their reality *now*. Anything could happen, but the remarkable realization is that the parents are not panicking or showing any sign of distress. This might not have been the case as recently as fifteen years ago perhaps. For my parents' generation, the boys may have expected punishment if they did not submit to wearing the heteronormative shirt and shorts. But now, the boys, guided by the wisdom of their parents, are being honest with themselves: their wants, their desires, their inclinations. This is the path children take when sexual attraction or activity is not even a glint in their eye; a child's behavior or proclivity gives us a clue into the complex sexual identity still gestating inside each of them.

Alan Downs in his book *The Velvet Rage* describes the often painful awareness in the gay child of being different than the others. He uses the second-person narration to draw the reader into a place of familiarity and solidarity:

> But perhaps starting at the ages of four to six, your parents realized that you were different. They didn't know exactly how or why, but you were definitely not quite like the other children they had known. It may have had little or no influence on their love for you, but they may have treated you in a different manner than your siblings, or differently than your friends' parents treated them. You too began to understand that you were different. The understanding was only dim at first. But as those early years progressed into adolescence, you became increasingly aware that you weren't like other boys—maybe not even like your parents.[2]

At a certain point, probably puberty, things kick into high gear for children. Identity flowers into attraction and impulse. It is unlikely that a sixteen-year-old male or female, for example, would *not* have some sort of semblance of an idea of where his or her attraction lies—even if it is, well, complicated. And for the LGBT+ population, by about age sixteen, no doubt, these boys and girls have experienced an all-too-chilling feeling and raw emotion: *I am not like the others*. Downs continues:

> Along with the growing knowledge that we were different was an equally expanding fear that our "different-ness" would cause us to lose the love and affection of our parents. This terror of being abandoned, alone, and unable to survive forced us to find a way—*any way*—to retain our parents' love. We couldn't change ourselves, but we could change the way we acted. We could hide our differences,

ingratiate ourselves to our mothers, and distance ourselves from our fathers whom we somehow knew would destroy us if they discovered our true nature.

And we didn't hide our true selves just from our parents. As best we could, we hid the truth from everyone, especially from other children. Children, probably more than any other people, are keenly aware of differences from one another, and often torment one another they perceive as different. . . . It was this early abuse at the hands of our peers, coupled with the fear of rejection by our parents, that ingrained in us one very strident lesson: *There was something about us that was disgusting, aberrant, and essentially unlovable.*[3]

For a queer child, the most powerful of bittersweet feelings is that sense that he or she is not like the other children in some way. This exposes that great human wound in the LGBT+ community that, unfortunately, separates them from heterosexuals in modern society. For on the one end of the spectrum, the consequences may be minor at best. Maybe the young person has to be more discreet in conversations with friends. Maybe the teen has to endure gay-related epithets from his or her friends for a period of time. Maybe the dreaded high school locker room will just be a stress pot for those few teen years.

Chris Glaser, an out Presbyterian who describes his path in ministry in *Uncommon Calling,* paints it this way:

> We grow up feeling bad about our sexual urges and our bodies because this early silence speaks louder than the subsequent words of assurance. A child assumes that what can't be talked about must be bad. Expression of sexual feelings among children and adolescents is usually met with parental anger or anxiety, because of parental protectionism and because of adults' own negative feelings about sexuality. All those children then grow up feeling

bad about their sexuality and their bodies and become adults with similar attitudes.[4]

This is just the positive upbringing. Because, on the other end of the spectrum, the situation can be downright dire. The child may be ostracized by his or her family; some may be abused, neglected, or kicked out of their homes; and most tragically, some, such as young transgender women, are killed at alarming rates in hate crimes.[5] At the very least, it would be impossible to find an LGBT+ person who at one point in his or her life did *not* experience some kind of feeling or emotion of being "different" that resulted in any one or more of these scenarios.

The average LGBT+ young person has had to do some extra growing up. Most have had to address their sexuality in a public way, such as with inquisitive family members or friends. They have had to move from a place of closure to disclosure, the most culturally familiar being the practice of "coming out" from the proverbial closet. But a coming out process (no matter how stressful, dramatic, emotional, joyous, or any adjective in between) has to necessarily be preceded by a coming out to oneself. It is that penetrating, soul-searching realization that can happen very early, that startles a person not yet fully formed as a human being into a major reality check: my life is not going to follow the path of my friends and family. And at some point, perhaps after years of living with that notion inside their head, the queer person comes out to herself or himself. A light switches from "straight" to "not-straight," let's say.

• • •

I knew something was up from about nine years old. Let us just say that puberty started early, and as my hormones signaled a sexual awakening like every other human being on the planet, my veins were decidedly filled with "non-straight" blood. By about age twelve, I knew my attraction to others was clearly not bound by gender. Therefore, I knew I was not straight. I knew I was not in the majority around me; I was not like the others. But it was later—far later—before honesty set in.

Like most young persons struggling with their sexuality, I learned to bottle it up. Downs explains, mixing tenses and person grammatically:

> We decided whatever it was—at the time we still may not have known what it was—must be hidden completely from view. Although we are older now, we are still driven by those insatiable, infantile drives for love and acceptance. In order to survive, we learned to become something that we thought would be more acceptable to our parents, teachers, and playmates.
>
> We made ourselves more acceptable to others in a variety of ways. Perhaps you learned that you could win approval by becoming more sensitive than the other boys. Maybe you learned that you could win approval by displaying a creativity that the other boys refused to show, or you learned to win approval by excelling at everything you did.[6]

In 2001, I went on a beach retreat in college with a bunch of friends, about fifteen altogether, a mixture of men and women. We stayed in a rental house together on Marathon Island near Key West, Florida. At some point on that trip, for whatever reason, the "light switch" I mentioned flipped over finally—some twelve years after I first felt *different*.

What happened was fairly innocuous. I had to share a bed with three of my male friends in this coed house rental. We approached this with democratic aplomb in this overcapacity vacation home: one of us takes the floor, the other three take the bed, and we all rotate position over the seven days. On day four, it was my turn to lay in the middle of the bed between two male friends. There, with flesh upon flesh innocently and platonically, I lay still like I was in a coffin, staring at the ceiling. I was terrified to touch either man by mistake or proximity error, for fear of arousal—emotional or otherwise. And yet, in this terror, in which I did not sleep, but only panicked, I felt another pervasive mood wash over me: *maybe I want that to happen.* The next day, as we all laid out on the beach, swam in the Gulf of Mexico waters, and chugged our margaritas, I removed myself from the crowd. I floated in the ocean on my back, head facing the beach several hundred feet ashore. Watching my friends chat and laugh, I floated and floated. The confusion of emotions from the night before was overwhelming. Was I resisting something primal about myself? Beyond that, how was I to decipher what was lust, and what was real emotion?

And then, on those gentle waves, as I drifted out to sea seemingly forever, I came to the conclusion that was, up to that point, the most honest thing I could conclude about myself: I was not straight. *Not straight.* So what does that mean? Gay? For a kid from the suburbs of Richmond, that was the only possibility, and it was also a dirty word. The effeminate boys in middle school were teased and called "faggot," I can distinctly remember. Even as far as into college, my roommates and I played video games and used the epithet in disgust to one another if we were to meet an unfair ending in *Goldeneye* or *Super Mario Kart.* I am certain I participated in that bullying and improper behavior. The realization in the great irony that I would be one of those "gay boys" was overwhelming; would I be bullied now too? Would the jocks suss me out? Would I continue to "pass" for straight?[7] Over the next several weeks and months, I sat with this information swirling in my head. The term "bisexual" became something to wrestle with, even though at the time it signaled some shadow assumptions, which I would later come to learn with some remorse. In reality, for much of the world, bisexuality is incredibly misunderstood and misrepresented. For many people, gay as well as straight, bisexuality is code for promiscuity, indecisiveness, inability to commit, and a halfway-house to just plain gay. More on this in the next section. But at the time, "bisexual" seemed the most logical description, even if I would come to regret using it to describe myself openly that summer of 2001. The heart of the matter was this: I was *not* straight. A new chapter in my life focused on honesty promptly began that summer.

• • •

Sexual identity really came into focus scientifically in the last seventy years. Without question, the pioneer in queer studies was Alfred Kinsey, an entomologist at Indiana University who in the 1940s switched gears to study human copulation. Sexual psychology was essentially born as Kinsey and his team unearthed a hornet's nest in human anatomy and physiology. In his seminal work, *Sexual Behavior in the Human Male* (1948), he worked like a taxonomist on human sexual behavior; one of his breakthroughs was about homosexuality. Kinsey noted that an amazing percentage of males in his studies had engaged in homosexual experiences at some point in their lives, and still others had unrequited attraction for the same sex. For some, it was in addition to their sexual desire toward women. Sexuality was clearly much more fluid than society had shaped it to be. This led him to the creation of the "Kinsey scale." The Kinsey scale was further explored in his subsequent companion book, *Sexual Behavior in the Human Female* (1953).

The Kinsey scale works on a spectrum, from zero (0) to six (6), that measures human sexual attraction. Someone who is a "0" is exclusively heterosexual; a man only desires sexual intimacy with a woman, for example. Someone who is a "6" is exclusively homosexual, entirely uninterested in sexual relations with the opposite sex. Granted, without the construction of the Kinsey scale, we might assume that a majority of society is either a 0 or a 6, with a growing number of people perhaps being a "3"—someone who enjoys an attraction to men and women with absolute equality (a 50-50 bisexual). The reality is that Kinsey's scale hypothesizes along a logic that most humans in society fall *between* 0 and 6. More people may be a 1, 2, 3, 4, or 5 than they would be a 0 or 6. It was simple math and logic to Alfred Kinsey. There are four bisexual-like options in the scale versus the three "cut-and-dry" options of gay, straight, and 50-50 bisexual.

Furthermore, a person may move along the spectrum at various points in their life, Kinsey asserted. A woman could go all the way to adulthood as a 0 or even a 1 or a 2, and then discover in her early forties that she now identifies as a 4 or a 5. This movement along the spectrum was essential to Kinsey's work. Though there are other studies and further science on the fluidity of sexual identity and attraction, I still prefer Kinsey's scale for its iconic simplicity. The malleability of sexuality may also shed light on our spiritual interior.

That leads me to that term again: discernment. *Discernment* is a major word with respect to Christian life. To discern is to make clear what is unclear, to separate out the parts or the elements so that clarity is achieved (as the Latin *dis- cern-* means "to separate from"). There is a general type of discernment, the kind that is intrinsic and in the heart, known only to the self and to God—indeed, it is the one I will illustrate next. And there is the formal kind, the kind that is a buzzword for a communal reality—a committee of peers, first and foremost. The step toward ordained ministry in the Episcopal Church traditionally begins with the formation of a discernment committee at the parish level. More on this in chapter three.

The other key term is *call,* as in the act of God speaking to an individual in order to start a conversation or to implore that person into some kind of service. It is rooted in Hebrew Scriptures, just as God talked to Moses and called him into action. Call and discernment go hand in hand: one is heard and the other is practiced. When a call is heard, the internal discernment begins, and it is followed by the external discernment, at least as far as the Church is concerned. It becomes a kind of vetting process.

The ideal phrase is *sense of call.* A "sense of call" is completely different from "my call." One refers to a hunch or feeling, wrapped in uncertainty. The other is naively certain. One is humble and deferential. The other is self-serving and prideful. Call is perfectly encapsulated in this iconic phrase from the original manual of discernment, *Listening Hearts*: "In responding to God's call, we discover ourselves."[8]

This speaks to the kind of integrity that must be a part of one's journey into discernment. It is a journey of self-discovery, much like the coming out process itself. And call comes from within, yes, but it is primarily a call from God to do something for God's purpose. I resist saying "God's plan," but for some people that brings great comfort. If the plan is to grow the kingdom of heaven on earth, to reorient our post-Eden broken world to a place of wholeness, then, sure, sign me up for that plan.[9]

Indeed, as *Listening Hearts* describes, "We are to become fully the people God created us to be."[10] The reality is that our sense of call is only limited by our grasp of what God desires with respect to our gifts or talents. The God of Genesis 2, who takes soil in two hands and forms human, *yitzar* in Hebrew, does this day after day.

God takes our talents and our gifts, our abilities and our limitations, and repurposes them for the work of the kingdom of heaven. By far the largest and most difficult step of this phase of the journey is to identify a sense of purpose, a sense of calling to something God-oriented. The next step is to articulate this to the community, and begin testing this sense of call.

• • •

In Christmas of 2009, I found myself in a pew of All Saints' Episcopal Church in Beverly Hills, listening to an offertory piece sung by the choir. It was the transition point in the Holy Eucharist, from liturgy of the Word to liturgy of the Table. We the people were gathering our alms, set against the backdrop of the setting of the altar for the Great Thanksgiving. The choral piece that day was timed for "John the Baptist" Sunday, which in actuality could be said to be two Sundays back-to-back in the season of Advent. It was "This is the Record of John" by Orlando Gibbons (1583–1625), an amazing call-and-response motet where the Jewish leaders implore John the Baptist to answer questions about his identity. John does not resist, but he recalibrates their orientation, suggesting that he is not a prophet, and not the Messiah, but merely the one who is preparing the way.

> And they said, "Art thou Elias? Art thou Elias?"
> And he said, "I am not."
> And he said plainly, "I am not the Christ."[11]

A switch flipped in me. It was unmistakably an echo of the switch that flipped in the waters off the shore of Marathon Key, Florida. I moved from shadow to light. As the choir sang the questions and the alto soloist clarified her answers to bring the identity of the protagonist into the fore, I was awakened. And it was exactly like the awakening of my awareness of my sexuality twelve years earlier.

I am not doing what I am supposed to be doing.

Okay, great. Countless millennials and people in midlife crises have had the same thought. What's the big deal? So change your job. Move to a new apartment, or a new city. Start a new endeavor.

No. This was not only bigger, but it was deeper in the soul. This was God speaking, if we can call it that. It was in the pit of my being, a sense that I was not doing what God wanted me to do.

I am not.

Some time after that brief stirring moment in the pews of All Saints' Church, I went home to Virginia for Christmas vacation. I was frustrated, I suppose. I spent the entire break confused and troubled. The reason was this: I had been down this road before. When I was fifteen, I went on my first mission trip with my Episcopal Church youth group to a very poor part of eastern Tennessee. On that trip, the twenty or so teenagers from a privileged section of Richmond suburbia lent their little hands to a Habitat for Humanity–style project. We built a bathroom onto the house of a ninety-five-year-old woman who had been too poor to have anything but an outhouse. She had gangrene and a missing leg. Her simple home reeked of old urine and mildew. And yet, she glowed with an inner spirit that was unmistakably holy. For in this rat pack of teens, she saw the hope that is founded on the light of the world. Because for her, her final years were about to be just a little bit better because of these kids. For her, the name of Jesus Christ had united these boys and girls and plucked them out of their privilege and into her dirty impoverished home to do some good work for a change. When we returned to Richmond, coming to worship to talk about our experience on the mission trip, I was overcome with emotion. What had just happened to me?

I was hooked on God from that point on. I knew from the second we drove our church van away from Jefferson City, Tennessee, at the end of that momentous trip, that I was in God's hands. I did not know how or when or by what means, but I knew from that point onward, I would be in the orbit of the Church. Soon there were other opportunities in my Richmond faith community to be involved, and the fellowship of those friends and that community stoked the fire of a kind of calling at this young age. By the time I was graduating from high school, the thought was crystallizing: what if I became a priest?

The priesthood seemed like a good gig. You work on Sundays, but how hard could the rest of the job be? Come to the office and read some books, write a sermon, maybe do some pontificating. Plan a mission trip here and there. Write a newsletter. Seems like fun, right?

The irony is, of course, it is not like that at all. But before we go there, I should point out that wiser heads prevailed in my case. I decided to think about the priesthood at a later time, and went off to college. The sense of call that was first stirred up at age fifteen would return again a few years later. That time, a college chaplain recognized a call happening in me, as I became a leader in our Episcopal Campus Ministry (that'll do it). But this time, for better or for worse, I resisted that calling. Instead, I abandoned what seemed like a sense of God's purpose for me, and went with the gut—which drew me out to Los Angeles to try to work in the film business. This led me to a career in marketing at Fox Searchlight Pictures, a division of 20th Century Fox. For nearly seven years, I was able to focus primarily on this work.

Lurking in the background all through this time, however, was a pull toward some kind of work for God's kingdom. But what does one do with a call that isn't necessarily convenient? We build blockades. If I can't hear God calling, maybe I can escape the responsibility. This was essentially what I, and many others, did in avoiding my true calling and my true self. Little did I realize, God tends to get God's way.

• • •

In Mark and Matthew's gospels, Simon son of Jonah, one of the twelve disciples, confesses in front of his friends that Jesus is "the Messiah, the Son of the living God" (Matt. 16:16). Jesus famously renames Simon as "Peter," *Cephas* in Aramaic, *Petra* in Greek, which means, literally, "rock." On this rock, Jesus builds his church. This is a little bit of redactic work on the part of the authors to emphasize and underscore Peter's importance in later becoming the head of the church. By the time of the composition of Mark and Matthew (as late as 70 CE and 90 CE, respectively), Peter would have been martyred and dead many years, but his influence on the formation of the early Church that would sprout Christianity would have been felt significantly.

The Confession of Peter, as we now refer to it, marks a moment in the New Testament when Christianity goes public. It ceases to be a following of insiders, and now has vested leadership in place for when Jesus the Christ will be killed, resurrected, and later ascended. Peter will ascend to leadership in early Christianity, keeping Jerusalem as a home base. Paul of Tarsus would ensure the Word is spread amongst the Gentiles in Asia Minor, Greece, Italy, and beyond. But Peter's importance has another dimension; he is, effectively, the first priest, bishop, and, by default, pope.

Part of Peter's legacy is that he was touched, literally and physically touched by Christ. Peter then baptizes and blesses others in Christ's name. He touches them, and they in turn touch others, and soon a line of succession is started. This is what we know as the Apostolic Succession, a belief that this system of hands laid upon heads in the ordination of clergy to this day stretches back by the determinable line of bishops all the way to Peter—and by transference, Jesus himself. The Roman Catholic Church, the Evangelical Lutheran Church in America (ELCA), and the Anglican Communion (including the Episcopal Church) all trace their bishops' lineage through the Apostolic Succession. This is an essential mark upon ordained clergy underpinning the theology of the clergy for two millennia.

The Apostolic Succession from St. Peter covers bishops (the *episcopate,* from the Greek word for "overseer") in the Church. Priests, deacons, and the laity make up the rest of the "orders" of the Church. Priests are ordained, and have been for centuries, to be pastoral and liturgical leaders in their communities and churches. The priesthood, or *presbyterate* (from the Greek for "elder"), is a call to administrate, officiate in the place of the bishop, and care for both rich and poor, sick and healthy alike. Deacons, who are members of the *diaconate* (from the Greek root word *diakonos,* which means "to the community") hold a special distinction, called to be on the frontlines of the world beyond the doors of the church sanctuary. The order of the diaconate compels its deacons to bring the church to the world, and then to bring the world's needs to the church. This takes a practical form to this very day, as it has since inception, as a role of holy servitude. Deacons tend to the sick, the poor, the marginalized; they are chaplains, prison ministers, and visitors to the infirmed. They assist in the liturgical and sacramental life of a church or mission, but they are not primarily concerned with the work of leading. They are servants.

The fourth, and arguably most essential, member of the holy orders of the Church is the laity. From the Greek words *laikos* and *laos*, meaning "people of God," the laity form the overwhelming majority of the faithful. Put simply, without lay members, there is no church. The laity are the people, the heart and soul of each parish. They participate and they lead mostly in voluntary capacities within the church—lead music, sing in choirs, teach, demonstrate good stewardship, assist where needed in liturgy. They count in the millions worldwide. In all of this, the laity discern their own calling in the Church and in the world, just as a prospective priest, deacon, or bishop.

When a person moves like I did after hearing Gibbons's "This is the Record of John" from sensing a call to testing a call (that is, speaking up about one's sense of call and testing its accuracy), the person used to receive a new title: *aspirant*.[12] As one might assume, this term was traditionally used to describe a woman or man who "aspires" not necessarily to the diaconate, presbyterate, or episcopate, but who instead aspires to lean on the community to assess where God is calling him or her. Now we might call this person a *seeker*.

All of this discussion of the nature of holy orders is the backdrop for the policy of the Episcopal Church in raising leaders—and defines how leadership is to be identified. Some key things are addressed right up front in the Canons of the Episcopal Church that should be in the mind of anyone approaching a test of his or her calling. Discernment processes are not to be denied due to any form of discrimination:

> Sec. 2. No person shall be denied access to the discernment process for any ministry, lay or ordained, in this Church because of race, color, ethnic origin, national origin, sex, marital status, sexual orientation, gender identity and expression, disabilities or age, except as otherwise provided by these Canons. No right to licensing, ordination, or election is hereby established.

Sec. 3. The provisions of these Canons for the admission of Candidates for the Ordination to the three Orders: Bishops, Priests and Deacons shall be equally applicable to men and women.[13]

Putting the polity aside for the moment, it is important for the discerner to realize a few remarkable things about the process for ministry in the Episcopal Church. Before a person even speaks up about their sense of a calling, a system has been laid in place that protects the person and the people of God. In a "postcrisis" era of the Church,[14] the need to have a stringent and thorough process in place for the selection of clergy is absolutely critical. This has put a strain on LGBT+ discerners, understandably, in a world that has generally feared the "other" and misunderstood sexuality of its people—and its clergy. Nevertheless, the Episcopal Church has a system in place that weeds out, at worst, psychologically or emotionally troubled seekers to ministry. At best, it is a system that rigorously examines and challenges the queer nominee to conform to the norms of a 240-year-old institution, as well as take seriously the need to be introspective and honest. This sets the stage, then, for the person's transition from one who senses a call to one who *tests* the call in the discernment process.

Notes

1. "Homosexuality 101" by Julie Harren, from *Facts About Youth*, a project of the American College of Pediatricians. factsaboutyouth.com.
2. Alan Downs, *The Velvet Rage: Overcoming the Pain of Growing Up Gay in a Straight Man's World* (Boston, MA: Da Capo Press, 2005), 10.
3. Ibid., 10–11 (emphasis in the original).
4. Chris Glaser, *Uncommon Calling: A Gay Man's Struggle to Serve the Church* (San Francisco: Harper & Row, 1988), 3.

5. For more on the media's neglect to cover this issue (including case studies where the victims' gender was obfuscated intentionally), read the fascinating 2018 GLAAD report "More Than a Number" at http://www.glaad.org/sites/default/files/MTAN/More%20Than%20A%20Number%20-%20GLAAD.pdf.

6. Downs, *Velvet Rage*, x.

7. The close observer of a young me in the 1990s would have noted that I had an affinity for Broadway show tunes, I had never dated a single girl in middle or high school, and, most telling, that I habitually videotaped the television soap opera *All My Children* and watched it every afternoon.

8. Suzanne G. Farnham, Joseph P. Gill, R. Taylor McLean, and Susan M. Ward, *Listening Hearts: Discerning Call in Community* (Harrisburg, PA: Morehouse Publishing, 1991), 2.

9. As opposed to "God has a plan all drawn up and I have to figure it out somehow."

10. Farnham et al., *Listening Hearts*, 2.

11. Orlando Gibbons, "This is the Record of John," 1600s, England.

12. The Canons of the Episcopal Church were amended in 2015 to focus less on self-nomination to the discernment process and more toward an understanding of call as discerned from the community. This has led to the abandonment of the once-familiar term "aspirant." However, it was so common to hear the term "aspirant" used fairly recently, as in my process and many colleagues' discernments as well, that it is easy to slip back into that terminology. In speaking in the present tense, I will instead refer to persons at this stage of the discernment process as "nominees."

13. The Archives of the Episcopal Church, *Constitution and Canons 2015*, Adopted and Revised in General Convention, 1789–2015, Title III: Ministry, Canon 1, p. 67, https://www.episcopalchurch.org/files/documents/2015_candc.pdf.

14. This is my term for an era going back about fifty years now, chronicling the rise of sexual abuse cases against clergy (most notably and notoriously at the hands of Roman Catholic priests, as depicted in the 2016 Best Picture winner, *Spotlight*). Note that I mean rise of *cases*, not of sexual abuse, which I am afraid has been going on for millennia so long as there are the clinically ill in positions of power over others.

2
The Historic Moment

> O my Lord, please send
> someone else. (Exod. 4:13)

One of the great moments of human relatability in the Hebrew Scriptures comes when Moses pushes back on God's call to him to lead the sons and daughters of Israel. Exasperated by the responsibility and anxious about what lies ahead, Moses demurs, in Exodus 4:10:

> O my Lord, I have never been eloquent, neither in the past nor even now that you have spoken to your servant; but I am slow of speech and slow of tongue.

YHWH, perhaps you've got the wrong person. I am not a leader. I cannot even speak in coherent sentences. What good am I to Israel? God essentially scolds Moses in a tone akin to a parent who assures a child that if she just sticks with it, she'll figure out how to ride that tricycle without the parent's help. God says, "Who gives speech to mortals? Who makes them mute or deaf, seeing or blind? Is it not I, the Lord?" Moses finally breaks and says, "O my Lord, please send someone else." God snaps a bit, tapping his brother Aaron to be Moses's voice. The dramatic irony is that we know Moses will indeed rise to the occasion under his newly ordained ministry.

There's a great deal of poignancy here. Not only does this exemplify the Bible illustrating the eternal *tête-à-tête* between God and God's creation, but it is also an illustration of God's persistence in lifting up the unexpected individual to greater roles. If the New Testament preaches a gospel of the oppressed, then it owes that attestation to the fact found in Exodus (as in so many other examples) of God taking delight in lifting up minorities, that is, not the idealized born-leaders, to leadership roles. Moses is one of many who maybe didn't quite "get" the call from God, maybe tried to demur, but as in all things, God gets God's way. And Moses seized the historical moment, however reluctantly in the beginning.

Early in the process to discern one's call, there will undoubtedly be a feeling of unworthiness. For some it will be as potent as the sense of call itself. Like faith itself, however, that doubt can strengthen the muscles and ligaments of calling. The Moses story reminds us that God insists on lifting up the unexpected in all forms, in all callings.

Nevertheless, it is far easier to respond to a call by saying to God, essentially, "You have the wrong person." This is amplified for the queer discerner, who would do well to ponder how much shame about her or his sexuality is confusing the sense of call. As call and sexual identity cross paths into adulthood, a familiar reaction can happen: the person at the heart of the struggle, the child of God, feels invaluable and incapable of assuming a mantle.

It is important first to name this, and to then realize that this is far from uncommon. In his provocative essay on God and homosexuality called "Unzipping Church," Thomas Bohache describes the response to call in the LGBT+ person as a problem of theology, or understanding of how God works:

> All of us bring our own presuppositions to the study of the Divine and Her interactions with Creation; likewise, we bring our histories—particularly our sexual histories—with us as we approach a God who meets us in our circumstances, even when we would seek to keep those circumstances private or secret. This God blows the doors off our closets, infiltrates our decent lives, and makes us take a closer look at who we really are, not whom we want the world to see.[1]

Bohache advocates for coming out, both sexually and in following God. This radical coming out is precipitated by the work of God through the Holy Spirit, a dramatic exploding of the closet. In the wake of this, God is unleashing our true selves to the world, and really wants us to be nothing less than who we were created to be.

But for the LGBT+ seeker, how can a God who inspired a church and, indeed, a society that has actively oppressed this minority (and others) for so long be the same God who wants to change its leadership from within? In other words, the Moses parable makes sense for Moses, but how can that Judeo-Christian understanding of God allow it to go radically further to a gay, lesbian, bisexual, or transgender voice of the oppressed?

At its heart is a conflict over a fundamental understanding of who God is and how God operates. The simplest spectrum for people of faith might be a continuum between understanding God as omnipotent, omniscient, and changeless—versus God as processional; that is, evolving, creative, and experiential. The predominant theological underpinning of the Abrahamic faith traditions, including Christianity, has been the classical account. So: God has a specific plan, knows all our thoughts, sees the future, and has preordained the path of creation. Problematically, this can lead many to suppose that God causes evil, oppression, pain, natural disasters, and the like. On the other side of the spectrum is the strand of study called "process theology" that imagines God as continually seeking. Like the related strand of theology called *liberation theology* (a theology from the view of the oppressed, highlighted in the work of Gustavo Gutiérrez in Latin American communities in the 1960s), process theology underscores that all study of God "emerges from our lived experiences of pain, struggle, and ... personal perplexity."[2] Inspired by the work of theologian A. N. Whitehead, process theologians have described this understanding of God as "grounded in experience and perspective," rationalizing that God experiences pain and love along with us and is able to change or adapt as such.[3]

All of this signals that an expansive understanding of God favors the queer person greatly. It opens up the possibility that God is not causing this oppression. God is not punishing the world in natural disasters for the sins of the queer community, as evangelical fundamentalists like Pat Robertson have frequently posited. Process theology opens up a window in which God can change; perhaps God is calling the Church now to be populated with a far more diverse set of leaders. Time and history would certainly point to this as likely. And ultimately, God, the "source of healing possibilities and compassionate companionship," is continually committed to lifting up these diverse and oppressed lives and voices into service.[4] The arc of time has shown that we evolve, we change, and we learn. The Church is no different, and it points to the possibility that in an ever-expanding appreciation of our Almighty, that God herself—the same God who became incarnate in Christ to feel love and pain at our level—is big enough to admit mistakes and make amends.[5]

• • •

THE HISTORIC MOMENT

It was nearly ten years before my John the Baptist moment of clarity brought upon by the music of Orlando Gibbons when I moved to Los Angeles to try to work in the film industry. At the same time, I found myself instinctively hunting for an Episcopal congregation to join. I found what I was looking for in the parish of All Saints' in Beverly Hills, where I eventually delved into many ministries and opportunities. At one point in 2002, I was in the choir, in the 20s/30s group, folding bulletins as a volunteer in the church office, playing guitar in a praise-and-worship band, and serving as a youth group advisor in a role that returned me to what initially beckoned me to the Church in the first place. Not far along into this new chapter was a moment when the sense of call beckoned again. It was stronger now, and I was older at this point. It would have been perfectly acceptable to voice what I was feeling to someone such as a priest, but I resisted at this juncture. This was now 2003, and I could not discern between being in the orbit of the Church (which I clearly enjoyed) and being a leader in the Church. By this point, my sexuality seemed settled and I had vocalized that I was gay to most everyone I knew. I recall a kind of last flicker of interest in something like discernment for the priesthood around that point in time, but I also distinctly remember thinking, *I'm gay, and it's just too difficult.* Gay people were not supposed to be openly gay and also priests or leaders in the Church. That was the prevailing attitude, at least as far as I was aware, as recent as 2003. Things were about to change.

• • •

As public establishments in New York City go, the Stonewall Inn on Christopher Street is like so many others. It barely passes for a gay men's bar. It is nondescript and homey. It is small, blink-and-you-miss-it, and in this day and age has nothing remarkable about it to distinguish it historically. But "Stonewall," as it is known, is ground zero for the birth of a modern political and cultural movement.

Up to this point in the United States, homosexuality was generally not an open matter to be discussed. For millennia, there were men and women known to be attracted to the same sex. Yet their lives were relegated mostly to the "closet," that euphemism that describes a lockbox of sorts preventing them from coming out, as a debutante might on her eighteenth birthday—a public unveiling in glory. Well into the 1960s, even as social mores were loosening in Western culture, people who wanted to date people of the same sex had to be careful. The nuances of flirting, picking up dates, engaging in sexual behavior with members of the same sex had to be done in safe public realms. So Stonewall was one of the major hubs of homosexual male activity at this time, and no one seemed the worse for it.

That changed on June 28, 1969, when inexplicably, New York City police officers raided the Stonewall Inn to place gay men under arrest for lewd public activity. The scene erupted, and the public reacted the next day with riots. Though not as grand and destructive as the Watts riots some years earlier, the Stonewall riots were, for a burgeoning community ready to break out, cataclysmic. The riots led to the organization of a march in New York City's gay districts of Chelsea and Greenwich Village to mark the one-year anniversary of Stonewall. On June 28, 1970, that march transfigured into something more like a parade and celebration. This was the first gay "pride" parade. Soon communities of closeted and open gay men and women across the country rose up to form their own pride events. San Francisco, Los Angeles, Washington, DC, all became central to the extrapolation of the new era of LGBT+.

THE HISTORIC MOMENT

As tends to be the case with the LGBT+ community, the gay pride movement was a few steps back (in terms of years) from its sister movements: women's liberation and African American civil rights. By the bicentennial of the United States in 1976, all three major culture movements were in full swing and had become forces to reckon with, now that the LGBT+ movement had caught up. Women's liberation had icons in Gloria Steinem and black Americans had a spiritual leader (and, sadly, martyr) in Martin Luther King Jr., of course. In 1978, gays and lesbians claimed their own martyr to front the movement in San Francisco city controller Harvey Milk, whose public openness about his own homosexuality and his striving for rights of gay men and women had brought national attention to the cause. On November 27, 1978, Milk was gunned down in his office in city hall by sexually confused homophobe city supervisor, Dan White. Milk's martyrdom due to his sexual identity helped to cement the LGBT+ community as a mature movement.

As the Episcopal Church had done before with women and African Americans, it cautiously stepped in the direction of support of LGBT+ persons. The General Convention of 1976 took the first major step to basically acknowledge the existence of openly gay men and women in our churches:

> *Resolved.* That it is the sense of this General Convention that homosexual persons are children of God who have a full and equal claim with all other persons upon the love, acceptance, and pastoral concern and care of the Church.[6]

The wave was not exactly tidal, but tended to go hand-in-hand with political persuasions, the cause being taken up primarily by liberals. It was hard enough at this point in human history, let alone in the Church, to even muster up the acknowledgment that gay and lesbians were human beings. Whether or not gay people could marry was a wholly different question that would be addressed decades later. Whether or not queer people should and could be leaders was even more of a nonstarter.

• • •

The immediate ancestor to the sexuality debates in the Episcopal Church was the ordination of women to the priesthood in the 1970s. This marked a major theological shift in the American Church that would stand in stark contrast to the far more conservative ideals held in other countries in the Anglican Communion. The General Convention of 1973 struck down the ordination of women to the presbyterate, but the next year the retired bishop of Pennsylvania, Robert DeWitt, along with the Rt. Rev. Daniel Corrigan, retired bishop suffragan of Colorado, and the Rt. Rev. Edward Welles II, retired bishop of Milwaukee, disobeyed this ruling and ordained eleven women to the priesthood (nicknamed "the Philadelphia Eleven").[7] However right in doing so, the Episcopal Church which "prided itself on being democratic, with authority held in General Convention" had allowed this to transpire.[8] For some areas in the Church, this was another example of a postcolonial, pro-Western culture taking over. In other parts of the world, the change was too fast and too shattering to their fundamental beliefs, even for a church borne out of breaking the rules.[9] It drove a wedge between the provinces in the United States and those elsewhere (let alone within the Episcopal Church). The matter was mostly legislatively cleaned up in the 1976 General Convention, which paved the way for women to be ordained in the canons.

Clergy and leaders were divided from the 1970s into the 1980s about gender equality as well as human sexuality.

With respect to sexuality, if men or women were queer, yet celibate and quiet, there was really no problem with discernment to the priesthood. The question of whether or not a clergyperson could be *open* about their homosexuality was handled more like a live explosive—slowly and carefully. There were outliers to the status quo, of course. In 1977, quite early in the process, the bishop of New York, Paul Moore, ordained Ellen Barrett, an openly lesbian priest, to the presbyterate. The pot continued to stir, and the plight of the queer members of the body of Christ seemed rudderless. Out of the despair of the AIDS crisis in the 1980s, out of those ashes, rose a kind of phoenix. There was one frontier for the quietly queer clergypersons to expand into: open acceptance and affirmation.

A cadre of strong voices in the form of gay and lesbian clergy were growing in numbers into the late 1990s. As one of those priests confided to me once, they all knew each other for the most part. They had secret meetings and caucuses. Even seminaries had secret clubs for gay and lesbian students that were exclusive and private. The queer clergy in the Episcopal Church yearned for the chance to be themselves as they fully were. Slowly the lips were loosened, and it was possible to find a parish here and there, usually on the coasts or in the epicenters of major metropolitan areas, where it was known that the associate rector was a lesbian, or that the closeted gay rector had a long-time companion (not just his "roommate").

Like most social movements, someone needed to advance the ball. The first significant moment as such was when retired Bishop of Iowa William Righter (then serving as bishop assistant in the Diocese of Newark under Bishop John Shelby Spong) ordained openly gay and noncelibate candidate Barry Lee Stopfel to the diaconate in 1990. This was followed by years of litigation brought upon mostly by other bishops of the church, including charges of heresy.[10] In a key decision in 1996, the Episcopal Church's disciplinary proceedings resulted in a decision that was the equivalent of an acquittal of Bishop Righter. It forced the Church to say unequivocally that it "had no doctrine prohibiting the ordination of homosexuals." [11]

And, like most social movements, there were setbacks. The bishop of Newark, John Shelby Spong,[12] in 1992, made waves when he ordained openly gay priest Robert Williams. While on the surface it was probably an understandable move, in spite of the expected controversy, it blew up in the Church's face. Williams, later the author of a memoir entitled *Just As I Am,* spoke openly and publicly (including in *Time* magazine) about his propensity for nonmonogamy. This was met with immediate retribution in the form of judicial review and Title IV charges. He was forced to resign the priesthood soon after. A lot of the blame looking back was heaped on Bishop Spong's judgment—no doubt exacerbated by his many books from a radical-left theological and provocative point of view. The feeling was the time was not right yet for LGBT+ leadership of the Episcopal Church. Two steps forward, one step back.

At some undocumented point thereafter, there grew a consensus among the queer contingent that if there were ever to be great inroads in the advancement of their causes, there would need to be a visible leader. It was time to think big. There should be one strong candidate among them to lift up to the episcopate, or to the role of bishop. This person should be the voice of a queer generation, a leader who could signal a new era in the Church as well as have the charisma and pastoral leadership to make the crossover to mainstream acceptability. All of this really does sound like politics, or in a certain sense, like the machinations of a record label helping a country star like Taylor Swift make it big in pop music. That's because, in retrospect, the call of the queer community to lift up Gene

Robinson to the role of bishop was unmistakably an echo of both of those examples.

• • •

Nearly three decades after the ordination of women in the Episcopal Church, the rule of order would be upheld in a democratic episcopal election by the people of the Diocese of New Hampshire. Gene Robinson was the people's choice to be the new bishop in 2003. He was openly gay and partnered at the time, a radical possibility for a candidate for the episcopate. But Robinson had served the diocese for many years, was not outspoken in controversial ways as had been Robert Williams, and was dutifully deemed the best person for the job of bishop. His election was ratified at the General Convention in 2003, and the vote of 64-43 (by deputations) in the House of Deputies was framed by Frank Kirkpatrick in this way:

> Many deputies voted to confirm Robinson not because they believed that homosexuals ought to be bishops but because they could see no reason for denying his election since it had not violated any of the canons or protocols for the election of persons to the episcopate.[13]

For other provinces in the Anglican Communion, this was yet another example of postcolonialism. The Western branch of the Church was overstepping its bounds in this brash liberal movement and were forcing the issue for the faithful who were not in agreement. This triggered the splintering of churches and dioceses in the Episcopal Church as well. It would lead to schisms of territory as well as ideology. Breakaway churches joined a federation of Anglican Churches (removing the Episcopal moniker) and clergy reported to bishops in Africa in defiance. The creation of one of the organizations of these churches would be known as the Anglican Church in North America (ACNA).[14] Territory battles became long legal fights over who owned church buildings and properties—with the Episcopal Church winning each of these cases.

And in the shadow of all the political and societal strife was the service of one man, an eye of the hurricane, who became a beacon of hope to the LGBT+ community. Robinson did not shy away from the limelight and used his position of power in the media to preach God's inclusive love. His consecration laid the groundwork for others, including the first openly lesbian bishop, Mary Glasspool, to the episcopate in 2010. These changes had a profound impact on someone like me, who had worshipped and considered a calling, but had given up. In response to my sense of call, like Moses, I demurred. God had to have picked the wrong person, because I was gay. There was no way I could be openly gay and be a priest. The toothpaste was out of the tube and it would not go back in.

Gene Robinson and, later, Mary Glasspool (then the suffragan bishop of Los Angeles and now assistant bishop in New York) changed all of that for me and so many others. Suddenly, we who were gay and feeling pulled toward ordination had role models. We had people who had stared down fear of change—and won. And now there was no limit to our possibilities: we could be queer, and we could be leaders in the Church.

But this creates a new problem: what makes me worthy of the call?

• • •

This intersection of the political, sociocultural world, and the religious polity of the Episcopal Church over the last fifty years is prologue today to the LGBT+ person's sense of calling to the priesthood. The sense of call knows no precedent, knows nothing of its sexual identity's community or its martyrs, knows nothing of "I can do this" versus "I can't do this." The call is God's and God's alone. When a person feels a pull toward serving the people of God, perhaps even as an ordained leader in the Church that once forbade openness of identity, it must be set to the test. This happens in the context of the faith community—the church or parish, in most cases.

The historic moment of now for the Church and for her LGBT+ children of all ages is that this process is freely and openly available to all who seek it. This is a radical table-turn from Stonewall. Now the process can be as simple as this: a lesbian goes to her rector and says, "I think I am being called to ordained ministry."

The rector, the priest in charge of a parish or church, is typically the first stop on the journey and process. While Title III, Canon 3, provides the encouragement of congregations, schools, and other reasonable institutions wherein someone's call may be discerned, the most common of these is probably the congregation. The person who approaches his or her rector faces perhaps the most crucial step in the process. If the rector does not recognize that same call, then for both parties, the best thing to do may be to not move forward. But in many cases, the likelihood is that the rector has *already* recognized a calling to some higher form of leadership in the church for this person. Even more likely, the rector may have even noticed that the person is struggling or wrestling with something. These initial conversations between potential nominee and rector are so important, not simply because the rector is the first gateway into the discernment process, but the rector will need (and ideally, want) to be the nominee's champion along the way. The rector understandably will become a part of the process him- or herself at this early stage, ushering or mentoring the person all the way to completion of the process—wherever it may lead. The rector will have a great deal of perspective in a parish, for example, of where the nominee's talents best lie. This again is why the historical moment of the LGBT+ contingent in church leadership is so fascinating. Queer people bring their own unique gifts and talents to ministry just as straight people do.

Queer persons are gravitating toward a more traditional understanding of being a part of the fabric of a faith community. This, like the recent changes on same-sex marriage, is an upending of the tradition from within. Matthew Vines, author of *God and the Gay Christian,* explains:

> Especially for LGBT people who greatly value marriage, family, and community, the legalization of marriage equality makes a major difference in their ability to be able to envision a future for themselves that makes coming out worth the cost.... Many of those more traditional-minded LGBT people are Christians. As they continue to come out in higher numbers in the years to come, they will likely cause the number of religiously affiliated LGBT Americans to rise, and they will also help to build a bridge for other LGBT people to re-engage with faith if they wish to do so.[15]

Gay women—and gay men to some extent—will find an Israelite-esque power in reclaiming or even usurping the traditions formerly reserved for straight white men. In other words, LGBT+ clergy live into their role as reclaimers and redeemers of tradition, but leading traditionally. There are few things more rewarding or endearing for the LGBT+ worshipping community than to see, say, an openly queer, black, female priest celebrating the Eucharist, following the rubrics to the letter and restoring the justice of the act by enabling it to be so. From all of this comes a sense that LGBT+ leaders in the church have a unique position as liberators of tradition by virtually reclaiming said tradition.

We have seen how the LGBT+ community has been able to navigate this historic moment. The beginnings of the modern era of expanded acceptance that began at the steps of Stonewall led to the new historic moment where gay men and women are the new leaders of God's church. The Episcopal Church is blessed by the presence of these persons, who can bring their own gifts from their experience into the fold. Getting to that leadership stage, however, involves a lengthy process. The stage of discernment at the parish level is designed to find the Teflon leaders of a once-divided church. We turn now to the work of discernment in one's community.

Notes

1. Thomas Bohache, "Unzipping Church," in *Queering Christianity: Finding a Place at the Table for LGBTQI Christians,* ed. Robert E. Shore-Goss, Thomas Bohache, Patrick S. Cheng, Mona West (Santa Barbara, CA: Praeger, 2013), 273.

2. Bruce G. Epperly, *Process Theology: A Guide for the Perplexed* (London: Bloomsbury, 2011), 7.

3. Ibid., 1.

4. Ibid., 5.

5. Using this lens on reading scripture, for example, a delightful study of God as change agent emerges. In the book of Samuel, God regrets making Saul king (1 Sam 15:11), for example. Later in Luke's Gospel, we are told that Jesus "increased in wisdom" (Luke 2:52), implying that there was a point in which the pre-eternal Son of God, the Word Made Flesh, had some learning to do.

6. General Convention, *Journal of the General Convention of... The Episcopal Church, Minneapolis 1976* (New York: General Convention, 1977), C-109, https://episcopalarchives.org/cgi-bin/acts/acts_resolution.pl?resolution=1976-A069.

7. It never fails that in the church, sometimes it is the rule-breakers who help advance a cause when they know the gospel is on their side.

8. Jane Shaw, "Conflicts within the Anglican Communion," in *The Oxford Handbook of Theology, Sexuality and Gender,* ed. Adrian Thatcher (Oxford: Oxford University Press, 2015), 342.

9. This refers to Henry VIII's dismantling of the Roman Catholic Church in England in the sixteenth century, the start of the Church of England, mother church of the Anglican Communion.

10. Josef Kuhn, "Walter C. Righter dies; Episcopal bishop played role in gay rights in church," *The Washington Post,* September 12, 2011, https://www.washingtonpost.com/local/obituaries/walter-c-righter-dies-episcopal-bishop-played-role-in-gay-rights-in-church/2011/09/12/gIQAAcbuNK_story.html?utm_term=.244cb358dcfb.

11. Gustav Niebuhr, "Episcopal Bishop Absolved in Gay Ordination," *New York Times,* May 16, 1996, www.nytimes.com/1996/05/16/us/episcopal-bishop-absolved-in-gay-ordination.html.

12. You might want to become familiar with Bishop Spong and his prolific body of work. In my estimation, as key a figure he is for liberation theologians, Spong is also, however, one of the notorious lightning rods of progressive causes in the Episcopal Church and beyond. Borderline heretical (some would say *outright* heretical) in many realms, Spong has almost single-handedly alienated many in the Church due to the radical approach of his work and ministry.

13. Frank G. Kirkpatrick, *The Episcopal Church in Crisis: How Sex, the Bible, and Authority Are Dividing the Faithful* (Westport, CT: Greenwood Publishing Group, 2008), 16.

14. As of 2018, ACNA is still not recognized as a province of the Anglican Communion.

15. Matthew Vines, quoted in Eliel Cruz, "LGBT People of Faith: Why Are They Staying?," *The Advocate,* September 17, 2015, www.advocate.com/religion/2015/9/17/lgbt-people-faith-why-are-they-staying.

3
The Process

You shall no longer be called Jacob, but Israel, for you have striven with God and with humans, and have prevailed. (Gen. 32:28)

Somewhere around the turn of the second century CE, a letter to an early Christian community surfaced. The Church in its early formation would adapt this letter into worship and, when the time came, into Holy Scripture as a member of the New Testament. The letter was rebranded "The Epistle to the Hebrews," a nod to the fact that the letter was distributed to Jewish worshippers in and around Palestine. It is an exhortation to these peoples, written by a gifted Greek writer lost to history. It is most likely not a writing of the Apostle Paul. The letter to the Hebrews is a letter about community: community of faith, community of Christ, community of one another lifting each other up along the journey of life. Using athletic metaphors and a high Christological assumption (the strand of theology about how Jesus is the "Christ," in this case advocating him as preexistent and complicit in creation as God's "high priest"), the author begs these early Hebrew peoples to be strong in their faith. He (or she) asks them to endure, for the reward will be great.

In this portion of the letter to the Hebrews, we find an interesting assessment of the faith community:

> Therefore, my friends, since we have confidence to enter the sanctuary by the blood of Jesus, by the new and living way that he opened for us through the curtain (that is, through his flesh), and since we have a great priest over the house of God, let us approach with a true heart in full assurance of faith, with our hearts sprinkled clean from an evil conscience and our bodies washed with pure water. Let us hold fast to the confession of our hope without wavering, for he who has promised is faithful. And let us consider how to provoke one another to love and good deeds, not neglecting to meet together, as is the habit of some, but encouraging one another, and all the more as you see the Day approaching. (Heb. 10:19–25)

It is a rich theological statement, but it gives us a window into the expectations of a Christian community. We are to provoke not hatred, but love—and good deeds. We meet, face-to-face, as a communion. Our role in all things as a community of faith is to always be present at the table—metaphorically and literally.

This is especially helpful when we remember that more and more the body of Christ is becoming complicated. For the LGBT+ discerner, there is a real sense even at an early stage of the process that the Church is a vast entity with people of all political and sexual persuasions. This makes the task of living together and walking together in faith all the more challenging. But it is clear from the queer perspective that this diversity, even when uncomfortable, is expanding and a part of God's creative design. The formal discernment process happens in the shadow of this task. It is shaped by the influence and participation of the community. It is true that a bishop has the ecclesiastical authority to bypass this process and ordain whomever he or she wishes to ordain. But this rarely, if ever, happens and bishops who were once priests, who were once aspirants, might remember the value of this stage of the process. For an institution such as the Church that concentrates on the pastoral lives of its members, it is only appropriate that the work of discernment begins at the pastoral, congregational level—in the midst of the people.

• • •

When Maryetta Anschutz, then associate rector at All Saints' Beverly Hills, heard me tell my spiritual journey up until that point over coffee one morning in January 2010, she used the phrase "wrestling with God." There are moments along this discernment path that stick out to me as a major turning point or moment of clarity: this was one of those. It is amazing to look back and realize I had no idea of the scriptural context of this phrase. What she meant was a call-back to Jacob's encounter with God at Peniel, a clarion moment in Genesis 32 when the patriarch physically wrestles an "angel" in the roadway. He demands to be blessed and to know the angel's name. It's a curious story, because the Hebrew text shifts from "angel" to "God" at a certain point, and Jacob, via the narration, realizes he has encountered God and survived. God blesses Jacob, giving him the new name of Israel—which means, you guessed it, "wrestled with God."

By far the best part of this wonderfully unusual story is that in the wrestling match, Jacob is injured in his hip. He limps forever as a result of this wound, and it is a mark of his encounter with God. Like a surgical scar for a cancer patient long in remission, Jacob's hip is a reminder of the wounds inflicted. When we encounter God, especially at high-stakes moments like Jacob at Peniel, we may be forever changed and we may also have lasting scars that remind us of our mortality and our victory through that encounter.

Woundedness is woven in to the discernment process for everyone. Likewise, the LGBT+ aspirant may carry particular scars of shame, guilt, and oppression, to name a few, on the journey of discernment. And if there is any doubt, let me say that the discernment process will revisit those old wounds.

I had trusted Maryetta with my story because she was about my age, had a solid sense of humor (that's important to me, have you noticed?), and was an inspiring preacher. She was the logical first stop on the train—I had to unload my story as it pertained to a sense of call, and see if she recognized anything familiar. This highlights one piece of advice for anyone in discernment at this phase: go find a deacon or priest (or bishop if you have regular access to one, of course). The reason is simple: it may take one to know one.[1] A priest, let's say, will hear in someone's life story familiar themes or beats. A priest can say with some surety that yes, the call you hear is real, even if it's hard to unpack. This is what Maryetta did for me.

She did the next thing of note, which was to turn me over to the interim rector, a bit of Episcopal polity that admittedly sounds like Luke being brought before the Emperor in *Return of the Jedi*. Mary Haddad had been the sexton at All Saints' Beverly Hills in the mid-1990s, then later a verger (the lay minister who leads worship and, as I now appreciate, herds bumbling clergy like Temple Grandin to cattle). All of that time cleaning the church property and serving around the altar pushed Mary to address her own sense of call. She went through the discernment process and became a priest in the Episcopal Church, serving at St. Bartholomew's in New York City and Grace Cathedral in San Francisco. Then after the 2010 retirement of the rector of All Saints', Carol Anderson, Mary was called back into the ironic and yet fitting role of interim rector of the parish as it searched for its new permanent rector. Interim rectors have fascinating jobs. The role is to fill a void, but also help a community turn the page. Sometimes this means making significant changes to personnel, liturgy, and programming. Interim rectors are mini John the Baptists, preparing the way for a rector who is typically vetted by a committee in order to meet the needs of the specific church.[2]

Mary Haddad brought me in to her office a few weeks after first "coming out" to Maryetta. That cat now out of the bag, I was feeling pretty relieved and like a weight had been lifted.[3] But Mary had me walk her through my whole story again. Even I was tired of hearing about myself, a feat I never thought possible. Mary's sage advice, I distinctly remember, was this: be prepared, you will have to tell your "story" over and over for the rest of your life. There was a recognition on her part that my sense of call was indeed accurate. I essentially passed the "rector" hurdle, that stop along the way where the priest in charge of your pastoral and spiritual formation has to identify and affirm at least the need for a discernment process. Mary left me with the promise of forming a committee over the next few months, asking me to submit names to her of just a few people I already knew, in order to fill out a broad-swath committee. All Saints' Beverly Hills had a bit of a discernment fever for a period of several years. Including Mary, about a dozen or so aspirants were sent on to seminary, and still others were given the "no" answer from their committee (see chapter 6).

In this liminal space of some four to five months, I went back to work at Fox Searchlight, and realized a change was already happening. I couldn't really talk about it or explain it to people, but I knew the ball was rolling. It wasn't clear to me where it was going, but it was a feeling of, regardless the outcome, a page turning. It was, frankly, hard to concentrate and be creative in a job that demanded inspiration and creativity. By the end of my formal discernment process, I would admit to coworkers and friends that I had begun to lose interest in my chosen career path. It is the first of many admonitions that the discernment process upends your life in more ways than one.

• • •

Discernment committees and, indeed, the process itself vary from diocese to diocese. Remember, the Episcopal Church canons prescribe this but do not give explicit instructions. In some dioceses, a nominee is immediately brought before the bishop.[4] In other dioceses, nominees are placed at other churches for a period of time to test out their call there. Still others begin with the Commission on Ministry first, and circle back to the parish later. But in Los Angeles, and indeed several other dioceses, the work begins at the parish level. For me, this meant that in a parish adept at discernment committees, this would be the moment when the call would be affirmed or not definitively.

In this scenario, a parish discernment committee works under the direction of the diocese. A diocese in the Episcopal Church usually has at least one staff member focused on deployment of clergy. In this arena, there is a canon to the ordinary,[5] who, at the direction of the bishop, lays out the diocesan policies for discernment. In Los Angeles, for example, this packet of information was given to a chairperson of my discernment committee once it was formed. To add a further helpful step, All Saints' had a moderating layperson who coordinated all the various discernment committees in process. That person walked myself and the committee through our task ahead.

The committee, once formed, is expected in most dioceses to work together for a period of six months to about eighteen months. There are usual caveats from all sides saying something to the effect of *the Spirit will guide how long the committee will meet.*[6] A committee might typically meet monthly, for example, with topics given in advance to be addressed. Or they can be free form. But the goals are generally the same: everyone, including the one in discernment, has to be asking themselves: Is God *really* calling this person to serve? Is the call specifically sacramental, that is, is it to ordained ministry? Is this the right use of this person's talents?

The last question is an incredibly useful one at this stage in the process. A strong discernment committee will ask questions, learn a bit about what drew him or her to God and the Church, and what kinds of things the person brings to the table. This is where the LGBT+ experience becomes even more sacred. In some cases, the stakes are higher for a discernment committee for a queer person. An affirmation of this person's call requires examining the person's gifts with a kind of removed indifference to their obvious qualifier: sexual identity.

This is difficult. Think about the classification of people into categories, the taxonomy of LGBT+ as mentioned in the author's note. Like it or not, our society is obsessed with two things: sex and the other. At this stage of aspiration—the space between sensing a call and hearing an affirmation or negation—it may be wise to start looking ahead to the possibility of one day working in a school, mission, or church. You may have already encountered or know of churches engaged in rector searches and the kind of profiling that inevitably happens. The white church really wants a black priest, even better, a black female priest. The church in the city that's always had male clergy really wants to show the world that it is diverse—let's find a female priest. The same thinking—which is human and often inescapable—happens with LGBT+ clergy. Churches may want a queer clergy person at some point, and that could be you. But how ready are many of our churches for queer rectors or vicars? The fact may be that as openly queer clergy, rector jobs will be trickier to find. They will likely be located only in metropolitan areas and more likely, on coasts.

These factors can be troubling and, in some cases, disqualifying for someone who is unusually focused on what kind of job they will do as a priest. The problem with this in the aspirant stage, as tempting as it is, is that it reveals two shadow sides of discernment for LGBT+ persons. The first is the assumption that no matter how comfortable you may be with your sexuality, the odds of your discernment committee—let alone a future rector search committee—being on the same wavelength are mighty slim. The second problem is there is an assumption that is ridiculously alluring at the parish discernment level: that this is a rubber stamp of something you have already decided with God. That is downright dangerous.[7] The last moment in which a discerner really has control over their part in the process is the moment of deciding to tell a priest you are feeling a call to God. From that point on, you are part of the machine, the process of the Episcopal Church.

• • •

At about six months into my parish discernment committee process, we had met together regularly once a month. It was largely convener-less, meaning no one person was facilitating. There were three people on the committee who had served on previous discernment committees, so they had a bit of an idea what kind of questions to ask. There was a lot of time spent having me explain my story

(Mary was right, you *do* have to retell your spiritual journey over and over). There were clarifying questions and follow-up questions:

> *What did you like best about youth group as a child?*
> *How did you feel God in those months when you moved across country and had to find a job in 2001?*
> *What do you think about during the Eucharist?*

Then we closed with prayer, mostly me leading the prayer to see what kind of words spilled out. I knew a prayer begins with addressing God, so I opted for the classical sounding "Heavenly Father . . ." and then to fill the prayer time I said something to the effect of "Thank you for this time together."[8] There's a pregnant pause. I grasp at words like straws to try to sound coherent in prayer. Then I wrap it up with something liturgical like "through your son Jesus Christ our Lord. Amen." If your prime focus in extemporaneous prayer—without practice, and in a denomination that is usually not that adept in extemporaneous prayer—is to sound prayer-like, then "through Jesus Christ our Lord. Amen" usually suffices. If your goal in extemporaneous prayer is to *actually* pray to God with and for others, then trust that the prayer itself is sufficient for God. Focus on that instead.[9]

But after about six months, I was feeling like it was all a chore. I liked the group a lot—some of them were dear friends, and others were people I admired greatly. I just felt as though our meetings were limping along, with little energy and rudderless.

I talked with another clergy member at All Saints', Gabriel Ferrer ("Gabri" for short, as he is known). Gabri is a gifted preacher blessed with a cognac voice and a strong pastoral sensibility.[10] He also famously, and somewhat reluctantly, made the move from laity to clergy after a long period of time as a verger, master of ceremonies, and lay preacher at All Saints'. Eventually God gets God's way.

I wanted Gabri not only to hear my story (plus I didn't know how many more times in one year I could revisit it all over again) but to hear my frustrations with the discernment committee. I said I was feeling like it was pedantic and wasn't going anywhere. And I confessed, over our entrées at lunch: I think maybe this was a big mistake and waste of time.

Without a flinch, Gabri's eyes bulged out of his head behind his glasses in delight—the kind of a delight a person shows when hearing a coming out and saying, "Oh, that's all?" He said, simply: "Oh, *that*? That's it? You're at the six-month point, that's *normal!*" He continued to fend off the feelings I was having in an incredibly reassuring way.[11] Everyone who goes through discernment falls into a trough about halfway through (the average All Saints' discernment committee lasted about a year). It's normal to feel discouraged, like you are wasting everyone's time, and that you are unworthy of a call. All that means is that it's "go time."[12] This is the time when you may need to find your role in the discernment committee. For me, this would be a leadership role.

But how do I take any control when God is supposed to be the one in control? This was my actual question, though I didn't want Gabri to know I was having such a rudimentary theological crisis; I kept it to myself. But it is symptomatic of the great question of the cosmos—is our life, is our call to serve, really a product of what God wants and controls? Or do we have some free will in the process? Do we have *agency* in discernment? Gabri's encouragement seemed to open a new realm in my thinking about this process. I can either sit back and let it take its course, or I can fix the rudder and insert myself into the process as an agent. The question of to what degree I or God were in control is wholly part of the process—this is the right question to always be asking oneself.

I returned to the committee the following month and tried on a more comfortable "uniform." I asked the questions. I told them stories about my spiritual struggles of the last few months and asked for their interpretation. I let them in willingly to my inner debate: am I cut out for ministry, or is this process all about heading to a resolution where I'm told "no"? In doing so, I found my voice in the second six months—I was a far more comfortable leader in group settings. The fact that I sat there for the first few and felt stymied and rudderless made perfect sense because, like it or not, I belong in the leader's seat. I prefer to moderate, to facilitate, not to offer the obligatory extemporaneous prayer but *invite* others to pray (which is exactly what I began doing). This may have been unique to my own discernment process, it should be noted; in many dioceses, there are more stringent guidelines governing how a committee conducts itself. But for me, this was an expansive moment.

The second half of my discernment committee was rich with discussion, theological and otherwise. We talked about my relationship with my partner, Andrew. We examined past problems and "red flags" such as times I drank to excess and regretted it. We shared our concerns for what kind of leader the Church needed—creative and passionate, sure, but someone who can unite the broad span of parishioners in the Episcopal arm. This energized my committee to prescribe some work for me to do: it was time to test my calling and try out some specific lay ministries.

The committee wanted me to try the Prayer Ministry, and the Home Lay Eucharistic Ministry (Home "LEM" for short). The Prayer Ministry consisted of lay volunteers who stayed behind after the main Sunday morning service to pray with those who approached the side altar in the chapel. Through this ministry, my discernment committee rightfully reasoned, I would be exposed to a priestly privilege: hearing someone's prayer request in the auspice of confidentiality. Plus, it would help me with the art of praying extemporaneously (I don't know what gave them that idea).

In this way, the Prayer Ministry helped me work through that gift of empathy, which usually has compassion as a component. I was sometimes heartbroken to hear the prayers for those in need. I would see the person who prayed for healing for a broken marriage or a cancer diagnosis or worse next week at church and my heart ached. I wanted to run up and ask them how things were going, but there was that code of silence.[13] Confidentiality is not hard, per se, but the restraint required to fight the temptation of being the person to fix everyone's problems is far more difficult. The point of the Prayer Ministry is less about a connection between the person praying and the pray-er, and more about interceding to God on behalf of the person. This is a significant part of priestly discernment: in absolving sins, blessing people, or consecrating the elements at Eucharist, the priest would do well to remember that they are merely one amongst many—set apart by the community to be the conduit of the people to God. More on this in the next chapter.

While I got my first test in priestliness with the Prayer Ministry, I was really baptized into basic pastoral care through the Home Lay Eucharistic Ministry. This lay-led ministry sent LEMs out into the world at the end of Eucharist, carrying a communion kit with already blessed bread and wine. We received the kit as part of the worship rite itself, a sending out to the tune of "We who are many are one body because we all share one bread and one cup."

The visitees were preassigned on a monthly basis, and I saw about six different people over the course of the next year and a half. They ranged from the very elderly to the very sick. What was most powerful to me was that, as an introvert, I could let the sacrament do the talking. In a pastoral situation, I started to see (and would learn to a greater extent later) that it wasn't about *what* you say. Indeed, some could not really communicate, at least, not at a normal clip. It was about the personal interaction, the meeting of a person in their moment of need, however great or small. It was truly being the body of Christ, by transporting the body and blood of Christ to the people who were in church in spirit only. It was me, a layperson, representing the communion or congregation, a person also set apart to fulfill a sacramental intercession—a priestly role in a priesthood of all believers. And it was a congregation saying to the poor, the sick, and the elderly: you are one of us. The rite of Home Communion, a version of Communion under Special Circumstances from the Book of Common Prayer, lasted all of five minutes. The pastoral significance lasted far beyond that.

I was incredibly grateful for my discernment committee's advice. It allowed me to report back to them that I had indeed tried what they prescribed, and found my role in God's church. If nothing else happened at this stage, I would be fine with that, truly. It was enough to be a part of God's kingdom in a serving role that didn't take a lot out of me, but reaped so many mutual spiritual rewards. My prayer life had deepened, my appreciation of the meaning of ministry for all had expanded, and my sense of peace with finding something to do to serve the Church was satiated.

But God wasn't done with me yet.

• • •

Like much of this book, I offer the personal anecdotes as one person's example of what a path of discernment looks like. At the parish discernment level, you will note that not once did my LGBT+ identity play a factor positively or negatively in where my journey unfolded. This is fairly unique. Los Angeles, and its corresponding diocese, albeit speckled with conservative heteronormative realms, is a bit of an oasis in this way. The reality for many of those who are entering into discernment is an experience filled with anxiety.[14]

What is it really like for a member of the LGBT+ community to feel a sense of call, and then face a committee for vetting? The answer is, by and large, extremely nerve-wracking. Feelings of unworthiness or shame—remnants of rocky coming-out experiences—are brought to fullness. For a person who has lived openly queer for much of their life—say, for a person in their midtwenties or early thirties in the twenty-first century—the examination of a discernment committee can be a challenge when they first encounter resistance to their call based on sexual identity. The Church, Spirit-filled, is made up of people who come at discernment from any angle with a variety of presuppositions and opinions. The discernment path begins small: just you and God. It expands to you and your rector and, in many cases, expands to your discernment committee. It will continue to expand, and as you add more people to the mix, you add more backgrounds and allegiances and, yes, prejudices. For some, the discernment committee at the parish level is anxiety-free like mine, a chance for the person at its heart to move past their sexual identity and really see if they have any gifts for ministry. For others, it can be a deflating experience where a person is startled to learn that people are either fixated on their sexuality (overly supportive being sometimes as problematic as unsupportive) or have hang-ups about queer clergy.

There are some important things to remember at this early stage. First, be at peace with this process. Peace requires some grace, too. God may have called you to serve in some way, but I am almost certain there was no fully written manual or blueprint delivered to your door by Jesus. How you will navigate discernment at the committee level depends on how at peace you are with the process. Perhaps the same God who called you to serve also orchestrated you to be in this particular place in time, with *this* particular discernment committee. If their questions are tough, maybe you will show resilience as you respond. If someone is hyperfocused on your being queer, perhaps you need to take it with grace. Or maybe there is a gracious way to say, "I'm sorry you are hung up on this piece of my identity."

Second, remember that these people make up the church. At this early stage, you must remember that if the priesthood is where your true calling lies, that you will be priest to *all* people. Even the ones you don't like. Even the homophobic ones. Even the wicked ones. And how you deal with that fact of life, even at this early stage, will test your mettle for the rest of the process. But gain some perspective, too. Just because people might intimidate or even frighten you because of your sexuality, remember that you can certainly correct them, in a sense, by helping God to change their hearts. I always believe that most people who are not comfortable with queer people (even those who are bully-ish and homophobic) need simply to get to know someone who is queer and eventually they will soften. I see it happen all the time. It is very difficult to hate someone you know. They may not change political parties or anything miraculous like that, but they will be hard-pressed to find negative things to say eventually if they have faces to go with the name-calling. Additionally, for your mental well-being as well as theirs, you should always stick up for yourself and call a spade a spade. So if someone is homophobic and in your committee, there's not much you can do except to call it out when it needs to be called out. Telling your rector or some other mediating presence is certainly a valid avenue. And there are times, I'm afraid—even and especially when it is less harmful words coming out of someone's mouth, like a complicit prejudice—when you do need to consider turning the other cheek as Jesus recommends. That's not giving up, but it is enduring for the sake of closing a cycle of injustice. And pray for that person. Because it is *their* problem. If you encounter a person blocking you from a fulsome discernment process based on your sexuality, and that person is particularly nasty about it . . . then I am not sure what you should do.[15] Perhaps ask for a new deck and new deal. But remember, even Eden had serpents.

But that leads me to the last step to accepting the anxious parts of discernment. You must trust that the system is not reduced to one person's influence. That is the beauty of the Episcopal Church and its discernment process. There are plenty of people who will jerk your chain throughout the whole process. But there are plenty, particularly in places of elected power—such as bishops and Commissions on Ministry—who have a better handle of what kind of person (LGBT+ or not) belongs in ordained ministry.

That next level, that level of bishops and Commissions on Ministry, is the stuff of a discernment process at the diocesan level.

Notes

1. Incidentally, I use that same rationale when people marvel at my astonishingly accurate "gaydar" (the ability to identify a fellow gay person in somewhat close proximity).

2. I intentionally give interim rectors the saintly connection to John the Baptist, but also intentionally stop short of completing the metaphor in making rectors akin to the Messiah.

3. Sound familiar?

4. On second thought, this is the more appropriate spot to bring up a metaphor related to being brought before the Emperor in *Return of the Jedi*.

5. *Ordinary* is one of those great winking ironic words that mean something more impactful in their root Greek or Latin form, such as this word meaning "order" or "alignment." But in English, alas, it sounds like one of the most unimpressive departments in which a person can be canonized for service. However, it is incredibly important: the bishop is the ordinary, and the canon to the ordinary is essentially the bishop's assistant.

6. Episco-speak for "We have no clue how long this will take, but hopefully God will let you all know at some appropriate point. And if not, well, it's always a human endeavor anyway."

7. Case in point: an aspirant in a church who received a *No* from the parish discernment committee. According to legend, this person did not expect or appreciate the response, argued to some degree with the committee members, and then changed dioceses. This is perhaps the worst-case scenario.

8. I still use something to this effect when I begin an extemporaneous prayer or a grace before meals. I'm not sure God is all that surprised to hear it each time, but it at least gives me a launching pad. And, I do mean it deep it down.

9. Practice makes perfect.

10. Never mind the fact that he is the son of Rosemary Clooney and Jose Ferrer, first cousin to George Clooney and husband to singer Debbie Boone. I said this was All Saints' *Beverly Hills*, didn't I?

11. Remember, I said aspirants can only help themselves more by seeking the advice of ordained clergy during discernment.

12. My words, not Gabri's. He's far more eloquent.

13. When a person becomes a clergy member, the Episcopal phrase is "under the stole," referring to the liturgical garment a deacon, priest, or bishop wears signifying their holy order.

14. Don't worry, my time for anxiety was coming.

15. Once on a flight to New York from Washington, DC, my husband and I were accosted for being, I guess, *obviously* gay. We were sitting next to each other doing crossword puzzles, I think (the

shame!). A woman who claimed to be a Baptist minister, no less, said, "The Bible says it's an abomination to be gay." (It doesn't.) We said something not so powerful like, "Well, sorry you feel that way." I was angrier no one around us came to our defense. But then again, I had an easy childhood, so this was my turn, I suppose. She eventually put a blanket over her head so she didn't have to look at us for the rest of the flight. I don't know if I could have reacted any better, but I wish I had said something clever.

4
Living with Authenticity

So God created humankind in his image,
in the image of God he created them;
male and female he created them. (Gen. 1:27)

The notion of being created in the image of God is essential to validation of the existence of the queer believer. From the very beginning of scripture, there is a poetic extrapolation of the created being as coming from the likeness of God. This is the heart of a macro-theological discussion surrounding the *imago dei*—the Latin term describing the relationship of humans to God. It is born out of a reading of the text of Genesis 1, which describes God saying amidst the act of creation, "Let us make humankind in our image." In this framing of theology, God still remains "perfect," and has borne this out by the creation of humans that reflect all of God's aspects. So the human has arms and legs, perhaps as God does, or sometimes does. The human smiles, displays emotions, feels love and pain. The *imago dei* underscores the idea that every detail reflects God in some way.

Now, assume you grow to maturity as a queer child. Your family, your friends, your peers, your society, your politicians all imply directly or indirectly that there is something wrong with you. As you grow into a sexually mature being, and indeed an emotionally mature being, you are conflicted to your core. Alan Downs paints the picture strikingly in *The Velvet Rage*: "How could we love ourselves when everything around us told us that we were unlovable?"[1]

The theological concept of *imago dei* is a glorious defense of existence for the LGBT+ minority. It creates an understanding of each individual's purposeful creation as God intended. As Lady Gaga famously said, "Baby, I was born this way." There is a real empowering truth to being able to claim this. The *imago dei* supports this notion, and it may be the fundamental lens of scripture that the LGBT+ can use in defense of our being. Chris Glaser explains in his book *Uncommon Calling*:

> I could affirm, with other human beings, that I was created in God's image. With other Christians, I could affirm reconciliation in Jesus Christ. The Spirit now led me into a future in which the only assurance would be God's presence in my joy and suffering. All this without renouncing the sexual orientation God gave me. All this without rejecting God's acceptance of me in Jesus Christ and the Body of Christ, the church. All this without refusing to follow the leading of the Holy Spirit in fulfilling the ministry to which she called me. I had previously accepted my ability to love another man intimately as a gift from God. Having integrated my Christian faith and my homosexuality, I now believed myself called to enable others to bring a similar integrity to their own lives and ministry. My ministry became one of reconciliation: to be instrumental in the Spirit's reconciling externally what she had

reconciled internally within me, bringing the gay, lesbian and Christian communities together.²

The launch pad for the LGBT+ discerner, and indeed any queer child of God, is to affirm that she or he is first and foremost made in God's image. Therefore, you are loved—wildly loved. The next stage is to take that affirmation and transform it into a life of authenticity.

• • •

Karl Barth, the great German reformed theologian from the early twentieth century, famously said that preachers in the pulpit need to have the Bible in one hand and the newspaper in the other.³ Discourse in the parish is usually at its most intense and Spirit-driven when it is juggling the written word in *The New York Times*, to name one example, with the proclamations of the gospel. A church leader in the Episcopalian tradition, ordained or not, is expected to continue the Barthian philosophy: it is essential to be mindful of scripture and tradition while balancing it with the daily headlines, Facebook posts, or tweets.

But at a certain point, any congregation, no matter how much it leans into social activism, can only take so much. And issues in the news dealing with human sexuality can sometimes dominate and overwhelm conversation. At worst, queer-related social activism with respect to prophetic preaching can risk losing the listener entirely. How does this happen, though? Should not these matters be always open for discussion and debate in the forum of the faith community? The answer is incredibly murky.

At this stage of discernment, it is entirely helpful to begin envisioning yourself in the active service of God in a congregation—parish, mission, or otherwise. This begins to open up avenues of exploration of the possibilities of ministry in the Church. It invites reflection about one's integrity and authenticity.

I have mentioned my husband, Andrew, in a sermon exactly zero times at this point in my ordained ministry.[4] The reason I give is that the lectionary thus far has not been conducive to me citing him homiletically. That is partially true. The reality, though, is that the line between one's personal life and one's ministerial life is complicated.

On the one hand, it is risky to make one's sermon about a spouse, or child, or family, and so forth.[5] This is where the discernment process comes raging back into the discussion. It is tempting when one is forming a call narrative to make the narrative all about the self. The narrative is really about, you guessed it, God. What does *God* want? Not so much, what do *I* want? What the self wants is not irrelevant, but it is also not paramount. As discussed in chapter 1, the sense of one's call is better termed "the sense of what God is doing in me." It is a sense of God's work in our lives. Preaching, among many other facets of the life of an ordained minister, is the act of opening up the Word of God (in the Holy Scriptures and in the life, death, and resurrection of Jesus Christ). The preacher is in many ways sensing how God is working in that particular moment to communicate to the people, and then interpreting that act to the congregation gathered. The preacher's voice is personal, as it must be. But the preacher's use of his or her personal life to illustrate what has been written in scripture has to be carefully navigated. So while it is true that a preacher has a right to talk about himself or herself, the deployment of such illustrations has to be done with great care and great restraint.

There are other complexities to be considered. Say you are the rector some day of a politically complex congregation (that is, one that has a pretty even split between Republicans and Democrats). It is true, though not by any means exclusively so, that LGBT+ voters skew Democratic and that the Democratic party purports to have a primary focus on the minorities of the United States. So what happens when the president tweets something marginalizing one or more of the Ls, Gs, Bs, Ts, +s? This in fact did happen in July 2017 when President Donald Trump tweeted a proclamation that banned transgender persons from serving in the military.[6] It was swiftly rebuked by the military brass who had not actually received any formal request from the White House. In three tweets of 140 characters or less, the president decisively ostracized transgender persons. It was fairly shocking and seemed to have no rationale whatsoever.[7] Episcopal bishops and rectors across the country by and large had to issue some sort of response, including the presiding bishop, Michael Curry, invoking the *imago dei* as a defense:

> In light of President Trump's tweet banning transgender individuals from serving in the military and the Department of Justice's argument that employers can legally discriminate against people on the basis of sexual orientation, I am compelled to oppose these actions and to affirm the moral principle of equal rights for all persons, including the LGBTQ communities. I do so as a follower of Jesus Christ, as Presiding Bishop of the Episcopal Church, and as a citizen who loves this country. This conviction is not born primarily of a social ideal, but of the teachings of Jesus of Nazareth and the witness of our biblical and theological tradition. Genesis 1:26–27 teaches us that all human beings are created in the image and likeness of God. This is a divine declaration of the inherent sanctity, dignity and equality of every person.[8]

Far more fiery responses came from colleagues across the Church on social media, to be expected. I myself exploded, and wrote a scathing, clever, Pulitzer-worthy response:

"The president is a jerk."[9] I really wanted to say something stronger, but even the idea of stepping into the political forum in this way revealed to friends, extended family—and yes, parishioners—that I was drawing a line. No matter the fact that the line drawn, from my theological perspective, was the same one Jesus would have drawn (he would have used more colorful, parabolic language, using some poetic Aramaic, I'm sure). I knew right-leaning parishioners might be taken aback, or take me to task. I knew Trump supporters would even take this PG-rated post as a there-he-goes-again-that-crazy-leftist-liberal. Some did. One unfriended me on Facebook, furthering siphoning us all into bubbles or silos.

The point of this is that words matter, but words from a priest in the Episcopal Church can carry weight. Censuring or editing oneself is a price to pay for the privilege of serving God's people and walking spiritual journeys with them in intimate, special occasions. It is not a license to tell them "I'm right, you're wrong." It is certainly not an occasion to force-feed people anything, political or theological, that they are not yet open to considering. This is the glory and the struggle of being a preacher *and* a pastor.

The reality of being an LGBT+ leader, too, is that, for the most part, people may only see your sexuality, at least in the beginning. First impressions therefore matter. A conservative parishioner may be wondering how long it will take for the queer priest to inflict his or her politics upon them. There is a great deal of fear from this perspective. It hits at the heart of what it means to be human: we are afraid of change. We crave comfort. And we adore familiarity. The LGBT+ priest is the epitome of change, whether or not they vote red or blue, own three houses or five guns. The LGBT+ priest is simply still an anomaly.

Already then, the task of living authentically as an LGBT+ leader sounds like a mush of difficult egg-shell walking. And, truthfully, it is. You can preach to the choir in a small gay community of twenty-five die-hard parishioners in West Hollywood or DuPont Circle or Chelsea. And this is completely fine if that is what you feel called to do. Or you go another route and *be who God made you* to others who need to have a pastor who can sympathize with their concerns, can take Jesus's great commission in Mark and Matthew's Gospel seriously as an LGBT+ leader: "Go into all the world and proclaim the good news" (Mark 16:15).

• • •

As we journey through the process of discernment, you may wonder at this point why the detour to how to be a queer priest in a parish. There's a reason for this—because the first affirmation of your calling at the parish discernment level leads next to the diocesan level where the question of authenticity is reprioritized. It also becomes bureaucratic.

The approval of a parish discernment committee is a huge hurdle, perhaps the hardest to pass in the whole process. But it is not the one that counts, ultimately, when we are talking about ordination. It is easy to assume that getting through the parish level is a victory that means the process is all rubber stamping from here on out. In some cases, this bears out to be true: the vestry of your congregation must sign a document to officially sponsor you for ordination. In fact, at several other junctures ahead to the point of actually being ordained a priest, a vestry will have to continue to sign off on your progress at least twice more (for ordination to the diaconate, then for ordination to the priesthood). The rector signs the same document, and each postulant is scheduled to meet with the diocesan bishop at a time mutually beneficial to all parties. I did say it would become bureaucratic.

And so, there I was, feeling proud and affirmed. A weight had been lifted, a ministry had been uncovered, and my future seemed to be changing shape before my eyes. My discernment committee decided it was time to write their formal letter recommending me for holy orders as a priest. It was signed and affirmed by the vestry of All Saints' and the new rector, Stephen Huber, who was generous in his support. It was hard not to feel as if I was a child presenting a straight-A report card to his parents. But moreso, I felt a sense of satisfaction that I was finally following God's call; now his flock was affirming that this was the right thing to do.

That's when I was told it was time to meet the bishop.

For many in discernment, mind you, *when* this happens varies. Some smaller dioceses have nominees in full conversation with their bishops at an early stage. Some bishops have known their nominees for decades. In my case, the diocese of Los Angeles may just be too large for the diocesan bishop to know what is going on everywhere. And since I did not grow up in this diocese, I was at a disadvantage. The bishop and I would be meeting face-to-face in a kind of job interview for the first time. That meant that he was going to probably examine me somehow. He would have get-to-know-you questions to which I would have to respond in the moment. Making it even more stressful was that the senior warden of the vestry and the rector had to be present as well. Suddenly this sounded like, at best, a presenting of a child to the tribe's chief at the age of maturity; at worst, it seemed like kind of terrifying warped game show.

I had three months to think about all the possible questions, and what kind of fool I would make of myself. This was also well before I knew much about my own bishop; Jon Bruno was something of a larger-than-life character. I mean that figuratively and literally. I am fairly sure he is seven foot seven.[10]

The universal claim about the bishop was that it was a labyrinth way through the diocesan offices, winding back through assistants' desks until you finally found his office. And in that office, he presided from behind a massive desk in a darkened room with one large spotlight that shone down upon him as if the light of heaven itself was shining down upon him.

But really the part of the experience that would give me the most anxiety would be the fact that I needed to wear a suit and tie.[11] This was not even a job interview, but it was already feeling like a deposition to a team of corporate lawyers by comparison.

The reality is that a nominee meeting a bishop for the conversation of discernment to the diaconate or priesthood is a significant moment. This is the melding of a nebulous, liminal space of listening to God's calling with the hierarchical tradition and polity of the Church. The Episcopal Church, an entity whose name literally means "bishop" (the term is *episcopate*), has based its faith and governance on the notion that overseers make the decisions for the flock. When a nominee comes before the bishop—whether it is a passing handshake at a retreat or a dramatic entry into a hallowed lair like my encounter—it is a momentous occasion.

• • •

In 1974, Louie Crew envisioned an LGBT+ community in the Episcopal Church. The group (of lay and ordained members) was later christened as Integrity. It is an incredibly apt name. The name is particularly helpful for a minority that has historically been greeted as abominable, immoral, and irresponsible. The work of the LGBT+ community in the last twenty years is to reject those old monikers. To be queer and to be a part of God's kingdom in Christ's one holy catholic and apostolic church is to demonstrate a new kind of integrity.

Integrity comes from the Latin word that gives us the mathematical term "integer," a number that connects one to another. To have integrity is to be integrated, connected, with the spiritual self, with God, with all human beings. Integrity is valued throughout the Church as the ideals and morals of a body of people who worship God are centrally located in the example of Christ—he who was without sin. For the rest of us, integrity does not equal perfection: there can be a hazy line between striving for perfection, and striving for integrity of oneself, as Chris Glaser describes:

> When Jesus speaks of being "perfect, even as your Father in heaven is perfect," the word translated "perfect" really suggests "maturity," in this case, spiritual maturity. Maturity, I believe, is the continuing integration of all one is, does, says, knows, thinks, feels, and believes. It is a never-completed process, if only because new data or new situations require fresh integration. The way we consider God as "the most . . . ," God would have the greatest integrity. God wills us to be mature as God is, which means imitating God's own integration process.[12]

Like other theologians who examine the relationship between sexuality and vocation, Glaser attributes being out to being integrated. In other words, the authentic self for the LGBT+ leader in the Church is the *out* self. As someone comes out of the closet, Glaser adds, "She or he moves toward the integration of sexuality with other components of her or his personality and existence."[13] It is likewise the same for integrating oneself in vocation and life.

The priest is supposed to model this for the congregation, in life and in work. This makes the onus on today's LGBT+ leaders in the church that much more difficult, brought to a place of opportunity in setting examples for others. The Catholic Church alongside the Anglican Communion has been beset by allegations of sexual abuse against minors, and indeed, they are not the only branches of Christianity to be culpable of this behavior. But the scar on clerical leadership is not going away anytime soon, and the latent fear that homosexuals pose some kind of harm to society may always linger in the minds of worshipers. The onus I speak of is for the gay and lesbian church leader to be mindful of one's integrity—priestly or not—because the people's faith is in our hands.

• • •

The bishop had a file on his desk, which had my stats, my photo, my essays, my whole application and life up until that point. I could see that it was open to some of my essay answers. He folded his arms and leaned back in his chair, let out a big sigh, and said with a half-cracked smile: "My brother, why on earth do you want to be a priest?" He proceeded to half-jokingly dissuade me from following this calling, which actually diffused some of the anxiety in the room. What followed seemed to me to be a giant pool of gobbledy-gook coming from my mouth. I was nervous in talking with the bishop because, as I later recognized, the stakes had been raised for me. I was now emotionally invested, as well as spiritually invested. To be passed on from the parish discernment level, having the weight of their confidence in my abilities as a potential priest was starting to be empowering—and overwhelming. For someone like me, it meant I felt a great sense of duty to the people of my parish in lifting me up for this role. I did not want to disappoint them.

This too marked a stark change in discernment from the beginnings. Early on, the task was to listen to God, be patient in navigating the unfamiliar waters of vocation, and test the faith in practice. Now the Episcopal Church polity was in play, and I was being subsumed by the tradition and its mechanism. On the one hand, if I were to fail in this interview, I would perhaps not be cut out for the rigors of the priesthood in a major faith denomination. On the other hand, if I were to succeed in this, I wondered if I might be so caught up in the hierarchical demands that I may lose that childlike sense of wonder about God and that initial calling.

So with all of these thoughts rattling in my brain in that moment, when I got to the final question from the bishop, I nearly choked. "Gregory, what makes you want to celebrate the Eucharist?" I tried to collect my thoughts into coherency, because my heart knew the answer even if my brain was not cooperating.

"I feel like it would be a great privilege," I stammered, "to be able to lead a congregation in that moment." The rest of my answer I simply cannot remember. I remember the bishop shutting my folder on his desk and kind of looking away, as if to say, "Oh, brother." What I wanted to say that I can better articulate now? That being a celebrant of the Eucharist is the *ultimate* privilege. It is the gravy on a feast that is strenuous by day, challenging in the soul, and strengthening in the long haul. It is a privilege to be able to preside at that table. It is an honor to break the bread and show to God's people once again that what was once one is now two, and four, and eight, and sixteen; that this bread is now that body, the people gathered before me, to consume and then go forth into the world to become Christ's body in the world. It would be a joy to pronounce these people absolved of their sins by virtue of their asking. It would be a culmination of my life's spiritual journey to be lifted up in all my brokenness, my imperfections, and my shortcomings, and as a member of a marginalized community on this planet, and be able to say "Ponder anew, what the Almighty can do."

But I did not say any of that. Because the truth is, you have to grow into understanding those kinds of things. In truth, it is difficult to articulate what beckons you to the Lord's table. I realize now that the bishop merely wanted to confirm that my heart was searching for answers—not the *right* answer per se (for who could know *that?*). But so long as I was a true searcher, then the process would not devour me.

"Well," he said, "I am going to give your file to the Commission on Ministry and approve you to go forward now." He then reopened the file and signed on a dotted line. I was searching for a zinger or a really profound thank-you as he signed his name, but instead said, "Now I can go on and do some great work for the Church."

On this line, his head jolted up and looked me straight in the eye with complete seriousness. "You already are," he said. "You're proclaiming the good news of Christ to the world every day in your work and to your fellow sisters and brothers."

"Right, yes." (Oops).

• • •

At no point in my process up until this stage did my sexual identity phase anyone. The bishop asked about my partner as if it was no big deal. My story is remarkably uncommon, because for most LGBT+ nominees, this is where the merging of hierarchy and sexual identity becomes treacherous. It is entirely within a bishop's prerogative to approve or disapprove a nominee for any reason or for no reason. In a more conservative diocese, the nominee may have been already coached to seek discernment elsewhere. If that nominee has reached the episcopal level, however, it is unlikely they will be advanced in the process on the simple grounds of theological disagreement. As for a nominee who has hit a dead end in his or her diocese, it is a time for a different kind of discernment: Is this calling strong enough that it would cause you to move perhaps and start over elsewhere? Or is it worth absorbing and making an impact as a baptized Christian? Either route would be entirely appropriate.

More concerning would be someone who aspires but who is not passed along in the process by a bishop because of numbers or job placements. Numbers may refer to quotas. In some dioceses, perhaps there can only be "so many" gay clergy, and therefore the dilemma centers on this being one queer nominee too many. More likely are bishops who are supportive of a nominee's sexual identity, but are faced with the more prevalent problem of lack of jobs.

For more rural dioceses, there are simply not enough churches for clergy. Filter in how many of these parishes are LGBT+-friendly, and the numbers may dwindle even further.[14] A bishop, as well as a commission on ministry, may be at great pains to consider sending someone to seminary and then having nowhere to place her or him upon ordination. At the same time, there are bishops who go to great lengths to lift up minorities in ordained ministry, often at great cost. Los Angeles was a competitive diocese for clergy, and though I would not have to worry about most parishes being anything but gay-friendly, I did have to worry a little about there being a job of any sort upon ordination.

• • •

To progress to the diocesan level of approval in the discernment process signifies a greater demand upon the nominee to share his or her life with the world. This is most tangible in the ubiquitous psychological exams. Every priest in the Episcopal Church must be evaluated to a medical and psychological degree. This is not to say that the results can be discriminatory, but they can be damning.

If the nominee submits to a medical exam, and he is revealed to be morbidly obese with Type 2 diabetes and other complications, this is undoubtedly an area of concern for the Commission on Ministry. The members or the bishop could be legitimately concerned about the health of this potential priest. There are many costs to factor in, not just hard monetary costs with the care of the person, but the challenges of a congregation coping with the person's illness, or worse, death.

It goes almost without saying that while the canonical process protects the rights of any person to enter into the process without impediment, the Church does not have control over an employer's right to hire or not hire a person. This applies to nominees in discernment as well. Similarly, if a psychological evaluation reveals a person has a clinically unhealthy history, there can be major blockades in the process. Certainly, some are obviously disqualifying: sexual abuse or harassment of another person, including being a registered sex offender; murder; misdemeanor drug possession; drunk driving episodes on record, and so on. And any of the following can most certainly be harbingers of a greater problem that could be a hindrance in advancing to become a postulant, let alone a priest:

- The nominee has tried to harm or perhaps kill himself or herself, and has not been treated by a therapist, counselor, psychiatrist, or psychologist.
- The nominee has bipolar disorder, with the same parameters as the first.
- The nominee has had several failed marriages.

- The nominee has a drug or alcohol dependency that is unchecked or untreated.
- The nominee has been reported for abuse of any kind.

While none of these are completely disqualifying, already it is clear that any of these, or any number of these, can be distressing for a priest in a supervisory role in a parish, mission, or congregation. This does not even scratch the surface of the other red flags, some of which have been complicating factors in various person's formal discernment processes. What if the nominee says they do not believe the Old Testament is legitimate as a work of Holy Scripture? What if they refuse to say the Nicene Creed? Consider the nominee who has never pledged in his or her life; worse yet, one who has never given a cent to the church, one who is not "known to the treasurer." Indeed, some sort of financial record is commonly turned over to the bishop or the Commission on Ministry. Perhaps this person has lied on his or her tax returns on deductible gifts. Maybe he or she is in massive credit card debt. These are all contributing factors to the assessment of one's integrity and his or her fitness to serve.

If all of this sounds alarming, it is because, again, the stakes are much higher now. The Commission on Ministry and the bishop are being asked to trust this person with the lives of their congregants and constituents. For some in the discernment process, the financial disclosures are a deal breaker; they drop out here. Others are implored to go to Alcoholics Anonymous. Still others are prescribed therapy with regular reports to the bishop. While not disqualifying by any means, these do underscore the serious nature of the priesthood.

And if anyone is an LGBT+ person and at this stage in life and vocational discernment, then for certain, some of these listed above ring true. The sad reality is that some in the

LGBT+ community *have* hurt themselves or attempted suicide. Suicide, the *second* leading cause of death for twelve- to twenty-four-year-olds, is multiplied in the LGBT+ community. LGBT+ young persons are five times as likely to have attempted suicide and three times as likely to even contemplate it as heterosexual persons their age.[15] The rate is even higher for the transgender community, 41 percent of whom have attempted suicide in their lives.[16] Many in the LGBT+ community, in attempts to cope with the loss of family or parents due to coming out, fill the void with drugs and alcohol—and understandably. Is that a total disqualification for the priesthood? Many have complicated sexual histories and lives that do not necessarily need to be fully disclosed to the whole world. Nevertheless, a psychological exam could expose some of these details and cause frustration on the nominee's part even while offering the potential of healing and reconciliation.

All of this plays in to this chapter's theme: living authentically. At this stage of the process, it is helpful to remember that the challenge in discernment all along has been to lead a life of openness. It may not be fair compared to hetero-normative nominees, to be sure, but it is necessary for the LGBT+ community. There *is* more work and there may be more to overcome, to sort out both one's past and personal "crap," so to speak. Being authentic to the world is the best foot forward, and indeed, the last hurdle at the hierarchical level of becoming a postulant.

There is another facet to the need to live authentically. While there may be fear or even residual shame from childhood about serving in a public capacity in the church, there is a deep intrinsic calling by the Holy Spirit to be *out*.

In 2010, a young college student at Rutgers University named Tyler Clementi was harassed by his roommate and friends for his homosexuality. Though he had a loving, supportive family, and an abundance of talents put to good use in music and education, Clementi was so overcome with the harassment and teasing that he committed suicide by jumping off the George Washington Bridge. When I first heard this story, I was profoundly affected. I had heard stories of gay beatings, such as Matthew Shepherd in 1998 in Laramie, Wyoming; but I had not had a connection with a victim of gay bashing with such a deep impact on me as Tyler Clementi. I suspect this had to do with the embarrassment and shame he felt. He likely had residual shame, perhaps guilt, for being gay and having to come out. All of those dark feelings—none of which came from God as punishment at all—swirled back up when he was externally bullied by his roommate. It could happen to anyone. It has happened to too many.[17]

At that precious time in which my discernment was beginning in 2010, I felt so strongly that Clementi should have had a mentor or a role model at his disposal. Someone should have been there to let him vent, to hear his concerns and fears, to remind him that he was a child of God and that he was made in the image of God. Perhaps that person should have been a priest—an out priest. A beacon of hope in a young man's difficult life. That was when the switch turned in me; it was clear that the calling was for me to be authentic to the world. As a leader in the church, we are called by Jesus to stand up for the marginalized and to bear witness to the good news of God's love. Episcopalians are incarnational, unmistakably. We stake our lives on the fact that God was incarnate in the life of Jesus Christ; he therefore knows our pains and the experience of our fears. He transforms us from the inside out through unconditional love. As an extension of the incarnation, we are called to transfigure ourselves to become Christ in the world. Tyler Clementi could have benefited from, and may have even needed, a queer priest who could bear witness to God's inclusive love. Instead, he had no one—and left to his own shadows he took his life.

Living authentically as an incarnational image of God through Christ's example, we are called as LGBT+ leaders to be ourselves out and proud. Yet we are really called to be our true selves. Parker Palmer, in his seminal discernment book, *Let Your Life Speak*, concludes this thought:

> Our deepest calling is to grow into our own authentic selfhood, whether or not it conforms to some image of who we *ought* to be. As we do so, we will not only find the joy that every human being seeks—we will also find our path of authentic service in the world.[18]

Notes

1. Downs, *Velvet Rage*, 1.
2. Glaser, *Uncommon Calling*, 46.
3. "Barth in Retirement," *Time*, May 31, 1963, content.time.com/time/subscriber/article/0,33009,896838,00.html.
4. Believe me, that statistic is not lost on him.
5. A book, however, is fair game.
6. Julie Hirschfeld Davis and Helene Cooper, "Trump Says Transgender People Will Not Be Allowed in the Military," *The New York Times*, July 26, 2017, www.nytimes.com/2017/07/26/us/politics/trump-transgender-military.html.
7. It was red meat for his far-right base.
8. Statement by the Presiding Bishop and Primate of the Episcopal Church, Michael B. Curry, July 29, 2017, https://www.episcopalchurch.org/posts/publicaffairs/episcopal-presiding-bishop-curry-i-am-compelled-oppose-these-actions-and-affirm.
9. I chickened out.
10. Or whatever cubits they used to measure Goliath.
11. I had never worn a tie to work in my life, and had been known to work at Fox Searchlight in linen pants, t-shirt, and flip flops.
12. Glaser, *Uncommon Calling*, 93–94.

13. Ibid., 94.

14. For more, including a map of gay-friendly congregations in the Episcopal Church, see http://www.integrityusa.org/welcoming-congregations.

15. Source: The Trevor Project, aggregating a number of studies, www.thetrevorproject.org/resources/preventing-suicide/facts-about-suicide.

16. John T. Reuter, "How a *Spokesman-Review* Columnist Twisted the Bible to Urge Bigotry against Transgender People," *Bloglander*, August 13, 2017, https://www.inlander.com/Bloglander/archives/2017/08/13/how-a-spokesman-review-columnist-twisted-the-bible-to-urge-bigotry-against-transgender-people.

17. The rash of LGBT+ suicides in the early twenty-first century prompted columnist Dan Savage and his husband, Terry, to create an online viral campaign called *It Gets Better*. Missional and, I believe, sacred to its core, the campaign was aimed at young persons consumed with shame and fear. Its message from celebrities and even a sitting president was full of God's love: You are loved and you are special. And no matter how bad things may seem, it gets better.

18. Parker Palmer, *Let Your Life Speak* (Hoboken, NJ: John Wiley & Sons, 2000), 16.

5
Priesthood and Sexual Identity

No good tree bears bad fruit, nor again does a bad tree bear good fruit; for each tree is known by its own fruit.
(Luke 6:43–44)

It is hard to wrap our heads around what kind of leader Jesus asks us to be.

Here in the Gospel of Luke, Jesus reminds the disciples that they will reflect him in the world. Track is laid for the humanity-as-Christ's-body-in-the-world metaphor that becomes the missional heart of the Eucharist.

In the late stages of formal discernment, it is worth pausing to reflect on the dialogue between the nominee's sexuality, sexual identity, and the priesthood of all believers. The intersection of queer identity and vocation, which is the entire examination of this book, really meets in the study of a modern branch of theology entitled *queer theology*.

It is helpful to remember the family tree of theology. From the millennia-old classical study of God, the omnipotent, immutable, unchangeable Almighty Father, there arose fresh accounting for what kind of creator God may truly be. In the post-Reformation, post-Enlightenment era of the last several hundred years, science and reason reigned supreme. Just as there was an abandonment of religion and eroding dependence on even the existence of God, there was a complimentary return on the Protestant side to a more personal and direct relationship with God—something the Church could and would not provide.

Out of this schism of sorts spawned alternative theologies, influenced by our reliance on experience and reason. One strand is A. N. Whitehead's development and articulation of *process theology,* which studies God through the lens of change and development. In this framework which challenges the classical account of God, the mind of God can be changed, God can evolve and experiment in creation, and God can learn from experience just as we can; the Incarnation in Christ therefore becomes a prism in which God can move from outright knowledge to a place of experiential love and pain. Through the lens of process theology, a new hope of the Church emerges, as Bruce Epperly explains:

> The church's openness to change is more than a matter of congregational preference or going along with social trends; it reflects the ongoing divine-human call and response present in every person's life and every community's history.[1]

The other major strand is *liberation theology,* which seeks to understand God's inclusive love from the point of view of the oppressed. Like process theology, liberation theology studies how God working through Jesus Christ continues to be a challenge to the infrastructure of religious leadership and the social norms of the "status quo."[2] Just as the incarnate Word of God was humiliated and executed on the cross, so too do countless throngs of oppressed minorities in humanity's history find an empathic God who liberates them from metaphorical and literal bondage—especially those infantilized by colonialism, white supremacy, patriarchy, and other sad realms influenced often by the Christian Church.

Descending almost concurrently from liberation theology are *feminist theology* and *black theology*. As it may be obvious by its name, feminist theology harnesses the aperture of liberation theology into the singular voice of women. A feminist theologian studies not just femininity and women's potential, although those are essential, but also the usurping of traditional male-centric domineering roles in the Church, society, and beyond. Thanks to feminist theology, which really came of age in the 1960s and 1970s, hearts and minds were transformed. Though it is nowhere near complete, the work of feminist theology paved the way for the ordination of women to the priesthood in the Episcopal Church and other denominations.

The experience of African Americans affected black theology in the United States in the shadow of the civil rights movement. Exemplified by the work of Union Seminary professor James H. Cone, author of *Black Theology and Black Power* in 1969, this branch of theology challenges hegemony. It pushes back on the assumption of one voice in theology belonging only to white persons. Echoing their experience in the 1960s, and indeed, the balance of American history, the plight of people of color has resurged in today's culture as a result of the continued oppressive violence (such as police brutality, leading to the protest movement "Black Lives Matter"), as well as a growing resistance to and awareness of systemic racism in white supremacy (that goes for *latent* white supremacy, not simply the more discernable neo-Nazis and Ku Klux Klan).

What may be then considered a related strand of theology borne out of these is *queer theology*. As presumed in that charming author's note, even the name of the strand of theology itself pronounces that it is a liberation theology. "Queer" for many decades served as the negative epithet for the gay community, until 1987 when news outlets started reporting images of Pride parades with banners stating, "We're Here Because We're Queer," and later, the far more chant-able, "We're Here, We're Queer—Get Used to It." The use of it as a brand on a tree of Christian theology reclaims the word's authority to hurt and transforms it into a label of inclusion.[3]

Queer, as hinted at earlier in this book, really encompasses a large and complex arena of civilization. In this book, it is being used as a label for everything that is not straight, or heteronormative. That used to be an assumption of roughly 4 to 5 percent of the population; Alfred Kinsey and other scientists in the field of sexual research have allowed for a tally closer to 40 to 50 percent—and that is just the reportable data. Queer theology was brought mainstream by the work of several key theologians and sociologists. The progenitor of the modern strand of queer theology was Michel Foucault, whose major work *Histoire de la Sexualité*, or *The History of Sexuality* (1984), explored power dynamics in oppressed sexual minorities (read: anyone queer). Foucault made the connection that after the term "homosexual" was invented essentially in Germany in the late nineteenth century, a sociological shift had occurred: from that point forward, a person was defined by his or her identity instead of with whom the person had sexual attraction or relations.[4]

So for a lesbian theologian, for example, the intersection of feminist and queer theology signals a rejection of the notion that all things related to sexuality in scripture and in tradition are already set and decided upon. There are no governing ideals or values in faith or in the Church that are locked in place, and certainly not in terms of heteronormative or male-specific patriarchy. Instead, "the God revealed in Jesus is one of love who looks for life in abundance and wholeness," and is not limited by any stretch of the imagination.[5] Boundaries have no power over Christ, and therefore there are no boundaries for us all, so goes the radical love argument of queer theology.[6]

Queer then, as Gerald McLoughlin puts it,

> is also the insult *turned*. No longer a mark of shame it becomes a sign for pride, like "gay." But unlike gay, it names more than erotic interests—a sexual orientation—and it names more than marginal, minority interests. It finds itself curiously central to culture at large, disavowed but necessary for a heterosexual normalcy that defines itself in terms of what it rejects.[7]

The plight of a transgender Christian is more complicated, just as the plight of the transgender community writ large is trickier. There are some who wish to reduce the moniker LGBT+ down to LGB, with a very rational reasoning: L, G, and B refer to sexuality and sexual attraction; *transgender* is really about gender identity. In other words, sexual attraction can and often works independently of one's gender identity. So a man who wishes to transition to female may be sexually attracted to women still; does that make her a lesbian? Or does that make her heterosexual? At the very least, in this book's parameters, it makes her queer. And so it is a mode of convenience to keep the T with the LGB. Furthermore, the struggles of a community that is defined by anything remotely related to their reproductive organs warrants a grouping together that provides strength in numbers.

The *T* in LGBT+ may not be going anywhere any time soon, but it is true that queer theology—like society in general—has a long way to go toward understanding and appreciating the transgender for all their innate beauty. The other binary-connected sexual minority, the bisexual, finds a different set of challenges stemming from further confusion in society and the Church. If queer theology helps us appreciate the human and the divine in Christ, then it follows for bisexual queer theory that there is a duality that exists in us. Just as Jesus breaks boundaries, bending norms by his very triumph over death, then the boundaries set by binary social constructs are knocked down as well. The bisexual Christian lives theologically in the "in-between spaces" as Laurel Dykstra, a bisexual theologian, termed it about her own joyful faith.[8] For Dykstra, Jesus "embrac[ed] the glorious ambiguity," refusing to be defined permanently and specifically. The bisexual theologian is more comfortable beyond the trappings of binary categories and sees an embodiment of this in the incarnate Christ.[9]

At the very least, a process theologian swapping lenses with queer theology delights in the intricacies and challenges the bisexual and the transgender individuals bring to the notion of *imago dei*. The transgender person asks, If God made me this way, and I need to transform my gender because I began life in the wrong gender, then did God make a mistake? Or perhaps this journey from male to female, female to male, is part of the process of God's beautiful unpacking of my own reality.

From all of this lineage of theology springs the queer discerner, and indeed, the queer Christian, who often embodies for the Church a society grappling with massive change in short bursts of time. For the once patriarchal, straight-laced, cisgender blanket of our world has been restitched into a quilt of vibrant new patterns. Queer theology thus embraces rejection of the established norms and principles, and the queer minister who follows the ultimate upender and boundary-breaker, Jesus of Nazareth, embraces this mantle in many ways.

Deposited into queer theology, then, is the queer leader called by God. In a priesthood of all believers, the priest follows the Christ who lived—and died—to destroy boundaries. With the wind of inclusive love at the backs of those discerning their call to ministry, the queer discernment nominee is freed to follow in a variety of paths, in a variety of roles, that may be presented their way.

• • •

In the final moments of being an nominee, the individual is under examination by the whole gathered Commission on Ministry whose main purpose is to oversee the process of admitting or denying aspirants for *postulancy*, usually in consultation or in conjunction with the decision of the bishop (who has the final ecclesiastical authority).

The word postulant has a brief history, much like aspirant. From the Latin word meaning "asking," *postulancy* defines the status of a person who is now officially preparing for holy orders: the vocational diaconate or the presbyterate. In most cases, but not all, a postulant spends a majority of his or her time in some form of higher education for ordained ministry, i.e., seminary. In this realm, whether it is residential (the student lives on or around a contained campus) or commuter, sometimes referred to as "distance learning" (the student does a combination of online coursework and brief intensives throughout the program), the educational objective is usually the master of divinity. The master's program, the MDiv for short, is comprehensive in its covering of the major canonical areas in which all priests must prove proficiency: theology, ethics, history, liturgy, scripture, and pastoral ministry. The choice to attend a residential seminary to obtain the MDiv full time is usually the one end of the spectrum; the other is to gradually advance in coursework part-time in order to sustain a living or second career.

The Episcopal Church has an array of seminaries in the United States. There are ten as of this publishing, and the ground is ever-shifting: Berkeley Divinity School at Yale Divinity School; Bexley Hall Seabury Western Theological Federation in Chicago; the Church Divinity School of the Pacific in Berkeley, California; the Episcopal Divinity School, formerly in Cambridge, Massachusetts, and as of this writing caucusing their degree program with nondenominational Union Seminary in New York City; General Theological Seminary in New York City; Nashotah House in Wisconsin; the School of Theology at the University of the South in Sewanee, Tennessee; the Seminary of the Southwest in Austin, Texas; Trinity Seminary in Pittsburgh, Pennsylvania; and Virginia Theological Seminary in Alexandria, VA, outside Washington, DC. Bishops and Commissions on Ministry, it should be noted, may have strong feelings about where their postulants ought to attend school. A postulant might, under consultation with the bishop and Commission of Ministry, attend a seminary of a different denomination (usually a decision based on proximity or commute). This would mean a final or extra year of "Anglican Studies" at one of the accredited Episcopal seminaries listed above. This program focuses the course work in one year on liturgy and worship, Anglican spirituality and theology, and those electives that will round out one's formation to be an Episcopal priest.

By the time a nominee has made it to his or her moment of evaluation for postulancy, the prospect of seminary will likely be on their minds. Because the stakes have become higher and the possibility of priesthood is on the line, it would be entirely normal and acceptable for the nominee to investigate a seminary. The notion of further education for the priesthood, if it is not already on the nominee's mind, really should be at this stage. It is essential and, in most cases, required.

For the LGBT+ nominee, the notion of going to seminary is understandably more complicated. The first concern is probably about theology. Seminaries of the Episcopal Church as delineated above cover a vast spectrum of beliefs and sympathies, as they probably should. An education at Trinity Seminary in Pittsburgh might be drastically different than the Church Divinity School of the Pacific in tone, emphasis, and some basic theological principles (such as the ordination of queer clergy). Just as not all Episcopalians think alike, neither do all queer persons. A lesbian may not automatically be happy theologically at Episcopal Divinity School/Union Theological Seminary (even though the stereotype holds that she will); and a gay man may not be all that comfortable at General Seminary in a historically gay-male enclave (also as tradition upholds). Doing this homework prior to meeting the Commission on Ministry for postulancy is actually a very good thing. It will generally not be received as being presumptive about an approval to go to seminary. At least, it should not be. It is, instead, something most Commissions will find admirable; this person is taking seriously the implications of their vocation and are trying to get a better sense of what the next few years of their life may look like.

It may help to pause at this point and unpack the postulancy retreat that is a staple of Episcopal dioceses.

• • •

The Diocese of Los Angeles is blessed with a large retreat center in Echo Park, north of downtown; a refined system of discernment polity and processes; and a thoroughly experienced and prepared Commission on Ministry and Standing Committee (the governing body of the legislative work of a diocese, ultimately responsible for certifying one's postulancy, candidacy, and ordinations). The retreat would be meticulously orchestrated and executed, for again, this is a diocese accustomed to juggling several nominees at once. There would be five aspirants at this retreat, including, with myself, two from my church.

At the Cathedral Center of St. Paul in Echo Park for my postulancy retreat weekend, I checked into my room. It was rightly the offspring of a monastic cell and a Radisson hotel room. Over twenty-four hours, there would be meetings, questions, information sessions, social time, and it would all climax with a two-hour period of waiting for the results of the Commission's decision. Indeed, as I would later discover, virtually every public minute of my time at the retreat would be graded and evaluated. This included a happy hour at the start of the retreat weekend: could it be they wanted to see who was coping with anxiety by downing a few beers rather quickly? Or more likely, the Commission wanted to simply see if their applicants had any social skills whatsoever (not a requirement, but boy, does it help).

We were likely evaluated on how we ate our dinner, even. The running joke is that the retreat center prefers to serve spaghetti for this first meal with the postulant applicants: a real test of ministry is how well a person can eat spaghetti.[10] But again, it was about conversation and interconnectivity.

The Commission concluded the evening with small group discussions, dividing us up to talk about preassigned topics in a format that was like my parish discernment on fast-forward. It may have been at this moment—never too late!—where I finally realized I was able to talk knowledgably about God to others. In our small group discussion, the question came up about how I view scripture. Not knowing very much about the Bible at this stage,[11] I nevertheless summoned a notion I had learned at All Saints' Beverly Hills: the Bible was a *living word*. I was not entirely versed in what this meant, but really liked the sound of it. As I began to prepare myself for a ramble to the small group, I instead blurted out some young theology: "It is not a dead book, but it is alive and still allowing us to interpret it all over again." It was not a very sophisticated response, but they could see my gears were spinning. I think it was a moment that really gave the Commission a glimmer of hope in me, as opposed to how I ate my spaghetti at dinner.

• • •

The second and final day at the postulancy retreat in Los Angeles was markedly different. Gone were casual conversations, light-hearted discussions, beverages. Gone too were the street clothes worn by the clergy members of the Commission; now they were all wearing their clericals. There was rumor the bishop would be there at some point. There was a small continental breakfast that screamed like a Holiday Inn: "Get out . . . fast."

The five aspirants including myself were split off individually and sent to various conference rooms. In each conference room, there were forty-five minutes of questions and answers from a selected group of Commission members to the aspirants. After four sessions, I had been talking about myself for nearly four hours and was now *very* tired of hearing my own spiritual life journey. The Commission asked a number of pertinent and not-so-pertinent questions throughout the day:

> *What sacrament do you think you would love to celebrate the most?*
> *Which seminary do you feel drawn to?*

What was the last thing you were listening to in the car before you arrived here?

I whirled from room to room and tried as best I could to answer fully and authentically. I remember too that I was blessed to be asked questions by a commission of clergy and lay leaders who really were not affected by my sexuality. They asked questions about Andrew, about what kind of support he would give to a possible change of vocation. I can only imagine what it would be like for someone to have to endure a Commission on Ministry postulancy retreat where his or her sexuality is a complicating risk factor. For that matter, I would also not be able to relate to someone who was closeted and going through this experience.

The retreat really transformed in the final two hours, where the five aspirants were told to wait in a refectory hall while the Commission and the bishop deliberated. While this part differs from diocese to diocese (with many waiting weeks after the postulancy retreat to make their decision and inform the aspirant), the fact remained in Los Angeles that the final say on postulancy belongs to the bishop in consultation with the Commission on Ministry. The small group Commission leaders who had asked the questions in each of our sessions would gather together in one large group. Everyone's copy of our "files" would be available and the floor would open for discussion about the applicant. In that room, the decision to approve someone for postulancy, the prospect of a three-year seminary education, and the radical change of someone's life to become a priest may be granted. For others, this may be the end of the line for any community affirmation of someone's sense of calling to sacramental leadership.

For two excruciating hours, I worried that I did not know what my future would look like. I worried that everything in our lives would change. I wondered anew if this whole process was a mistake. I feared the backlash of being openly queer and openly priested. Like a new letter on the LGBT+ acronym, was I creating a new identity for myself, something that would alienate me from a far larger majority: would I be *a gay priest*?

In those two prayerful hours,[12] I struggled to remember that this process was just that: a process that would determine where I *belong*. A *no* from the Commission on Ministry would not necessarily be a *no* from God, just a *no* to the priesthood. I had to trust that God would make it clear at some point what I was supposed to be doing with my life.

But for the moment, the waiting was terrible.

Notes

1. Epperly, *Process Theology*, 121.

2. Ibid., 122.

3. Patrick S. Cheng, *Radical Love: Introduction to Queer Theology* (New York: Seabury Books, 2011), 5.

4. Ibid., 7.

5. Lisa Isherwood, "Lesbians," in *The Oxford Handbook of Theology, Sexuality, and Gender*, ed. Adrian Thatcher (New York: Oxford University Press, 2014), 624.

6. Cheng, *Radical Love*, 79.

7. Gerard Loughlin, "Introduction," in *Queer Theology: Rethinking the Western Body*, ed. Gerard Loughlin (Malden, MA: Blackwell Publishing, 2007), 8.

8. Laurel Dykstra, "Jesus, Bread, Wine and Roses: A Bisexual Feminist at the Catholic Worker," in *Blessed Bi Spirit: Bisexual People of Faith*, ed. Debra R. Kolodny (New York: Continuum, 2000), 78–79, 87.

9. Accordingly, with a book about sexual and spiritual honesty, I discerned relatively recently that I am a "4" on the Kinsey scale. I am bisexual. Being attracted to men and women sexually does not preclude me from the inevitable that I would find one partner—mine happened to be a man.

10. Refusing to be confined by society's constructs, I prefer to swirl, slurp, and bite, spraying marinara sauce everywhere.

11. Fear not, you will get to know the Bible intimately if you make it to seminary. No one said you had to be an expert on the Bible before postulancy or seminary.

12. For me, pacing, sweating, and muttering expletives counts as prayer since I have invited God to be present.

6
No and Not Yet

Why do you look for the living among the dead?
(Luke 24:5)

Luke's Gospel is the only place in scripture where these chilling words are uttered. The women, Mary Magdalene, Salome, and the other Mary have come to the tomb of Jesus to anoint his body with fragrant oils. Just forty-eight hours earlier, they watched their Lord be crucified like a common bandit. Now he lay in Joseph of Arimathea's tomb with all hope of salvation seemingly lost. But that Easter miracle has begun: the tomb is found by the women to be empty. They stumble outside in a fog, wondering what on earth is happening. They are "perplexed," the text says. Just then a gardener in the cemetery shouts out to them cryptically: "Why do you look for the living among the dead?" Do you not understand? This is not the end of the story by any stretch. And like it or not, the Jesus you seek is not among the dead—not at all. He is risen.

In this moment, the perplexed women are on the front lines of a spiritual awakening. In this time of great despair, of utter darkness, there is a light breaking forth on that glorious early morning. There is hope.

• • •

The nominee has at this stage gone to the brink of self-examination and back. Each has submitted to psychological evaluations, introspective conversations galore, and examination by a bishop and a Commission on Ministry. They have been presented, tested, and reviewed. They carry with them a hope of a parish community that they have lifted up a new priest or deacon. They also carry with them that sense that their own personal call has been affirmed and recognized as true.

In all of this, it has come down to a few deliberative weeks, hours, maybe even minutes. The Commission representative, perhaps the appointed shepherd, perhaps the bishop, will make contact in person or by phone to affirm or reject the call. However, in this scenario, there are two possible answers of negation.

"Not now."

The other is "No."

It is really difficult as a human being to take a *No* answer as anything but outright rejection. It is so hard in the discernment process to *not* have the feeling of being passed over for a job. Except that feeling is amplified in some ways. It is not about a job that pays bills—it's far greater than that. This is about a vocation. This is about a way of life and place in the ranks of the Church hierarchy.

How can this *not* be a rejection?

• • •

When I waited to hear my response from the Commission on Ministry on an April morning in 2012, I had about two hours to process the possible results. I steeled myself for the *No* answer.

Andrew and I had spent the previous weekend wine tasting with friends in the Santa Barbara wine country near Los Olivos, California. It was a wonderful moment of escape, forgetting about the pressures of life and the reality that a change was imminent—even if the nature and design of that life change was uncertain. On the drive back to home in Los Angeles, I hit upon a breakthrough. Keeping Nora Gallagher's book *Practicing Resurrection* in my mind, I had to rethink what a *No* meant. It wasn't about rejection, no matter how tempting it was to feel that way. It was about redirection. Reorientation. Sure, the idea of being able to baptize a new person into the body of Christ, to marry a couple, to celebrate the Eucharist, were dangling out in front my face as a real possibility now. And while I felt beckoned to the proverbial and literal table, I had to prepare for the legitimate reality that a community of peers might not share that sentiment. This is that moment we all face where character shines through or is formed—how would I reorient my emotions and my calling?

I had long had an affinity for wine, not just for its deliciousness and its other tangible qualities. I loved the process. I loved the long months and years of raising grapes, finding the right climates, the delicacy of harvesting, pounding grapes, fermenting. Then the waiting. The years of barreling and patiently allowing the flavors and the alcohol to do their work. Only then is the tasting. It is hard not to realize the spiritual implications of wine-making. The fostering and growth is akin to the journey in faith we all take. Sometimes our bottle of wine is just not ready to be consumed.

It hit me like a lightning bolt on that drive back: if I receive a *No* answer, we would move to wine country and become vintners. That's right: give up my job (which was about to become more lucrative—not an easy decision to sit with). I would of course remain in the orbit of the church, perhaps worshipping and serving at St. Mark's in-the-Valley, Los Olivos. We would adopt and start a family.

But that would be just the day job. I would—*we* would—commit our lives to the Church as lay members. We would join St. Mark's-in-the-Valley, the Episcopal Church where our union was blessed in 2011. There we would hope to become a vital part of the laity: singing in the choir, helping in outreach, maybe running for vestry someday. The *No* answer would be merely a *No* to *ordained* ministry, not a *No* to ministry. My baptismal covenant would remain the same as it had when I was twelve weeks old: I would serve God in the Church in some manner that did not have to be deduced to ordained responsibility. I would be Christ in the world, whatever job or career I might have, whatever the journey. And, truly, all would be well.

Once I came to this decision on that drive back to Los Angeles, I felt much more at peace. The retreat weekend with the Commission on Ministry loomed, but I felt assured that God would look out for me one way or another. The peace that I felt through that prayerful drive home reminded me that the discernment process would not be a Pass/Fail vote, but merely a moment of clarity on the journey.

• • •

As alluded to in previous chapters and footnotes, there are a number of ways a person can receive this *No* response. My solution was to prepare myself to recognize the moment as a transition. I came to a place of peace in the anxious eye of a hurricane, realizing that no matter what would happen, it was time to collapse the current tent and move on to something else. This is an unmistakable act of the Holy Spirit. This is also the difficult phase where we must grapple with the term "the work of the Spirit."

NO AND NOT YET

For others, however, the *No* response can be quite shocking. It may come as a surprise. All of the preparatory work, the self-examination, the conversation, the wondering, and the pontificating seem to have been all for naught—if priesthood was the end goal, that is.

The end of my Commission on Ministry retreat weekend concluded with the revelations of the committee's decisions. Just as I was pulled in to a conference room to hear the results of my evaluation, I was witness to the moments *after* the results for my colleagues. In our group of six aspirants, two of us (including myself) were a *Yes* answer to postulancy. Two were *No* outright. I briefly passed one member of my cohort as he was processing the news with his rector nearby. She had her hands on his shoulders, looking him directly in the eye as if to calm down a child about to have a meltdown. I could hear her say "It's fine, we'll get through this . . ." as I passed by and continued walking down the hallway. In that moment, I both ached for his pain—and felt relieved that my morning had gone a bit differently. But it was my assumption that something about his process, and ultimately, the nonaffirmation of the priesthood as his calling to ministry, had blindsided him.

Again, the *No* answer at first may seem like a failure. The Church tries to counterbalance this thinking; the empowerment of the laity for leadership has been a driving focus in the last several decades as a fulsome understanding of what it means to be baptized Christian. But the system in which decisions are made on a hierarchical level, in a church in which hierarchy is part of its DNA, is bound to leave people disappointed on some level. The problem with the final answer prior to postulancy is that the stakes are just too high. For some, it has been a possibility that is all too tantalizing. A nominee can imagine herself on the path to the priesthood and the affirmation of so many committees, individuals, family members, and even bishops can be intoxicating. The final decision of a Commission on Ministry, or a bishop, can be almost devastating to those who feel a call to ordained ministry strongly.

For the LGBT+ nominee, the decision of a diocese to approve the person for postulancy is fraught with the complexities of sexuality. The question of whether the Commission on Ministry evaluated the person on the terms of their sexual identity is bound to be at the forefront. The nominee in some dioceses may get a raw deal, frankly. The possibility after the *No* answer is limited but not without hope. He or she may strongly consider trying again, through another diocese. This is challenging on many levels, and yet many nominees do this for many reasons. Sometimes the sense of call to the priesthood is so great that it is understandable that one may feel he or she did not present themselves in the best light; that he or she was given an unfair shake; or that simply this person is not fit to serve in *that* particular diocese; in other words, he or she is a victim of geography. The challenging aspect to this is discerning whether or not the Commission's *No* answer was rightfully administered. On some level, a nominee may have been waffling about this calling to begin with; perhaps the Commission picked up on this. Perhaps the person has too many challenges to overcome: addictions, depression, relationship issues, and the like. None of these are disqualifying on the surface, but if a Commission of peers is perceiving these to be overwhelmingly problematic, then this may have been a case of "close call."

Now sometimes the Commission on Ministry and the bishop may rightfully discern that the nominee's gifts are better served as a member of the laity. The church desperately needs lay leaders in all things nonsacramental (and some assistance on the sacramental, for that matter). If the system is working, the Commission will be taking into account the whole of the nominee's discernment journey and may be lifting up this person for important lay ministry. That ministry may have a function specifically in a church or congregation, or, more likely, in the world beyond the church. Indeed, one's vocation in any number of paths chosen—business, medical, service, teaching, and countless others—may be further informed by his or her ministerial gifts.

Nominees from the LBGT+ community by and large may take the *No* answer as a failure of the system, and this would not necessarily be wrong. The first recourse in this situation is to go to the last point of approval, usually the vestry or the rector of the sponsoring parish. The rector will know whether your gifts were rightfully acknowledged; and a savvy rector will be able to discern whether or not the nominee was given a fair shake.

If the rector and the parish affirm the *No* answer, and this is certainly possible (although it has the potential to reflect poorly on the rector and parish's decision to sponsor the nominee to the diocese in the first place!), there are recourses. This means moving and starting over elsewhere. Changing dioceses and starting over is taxing on the diocese, the parish (that would be a *new* parish in most cases), the Commission on Ministry (again, a *new one*), and the self. But if the sense of call is that strong and that warranted, perhaps this could be the work of the Spirit. The wilderness metaphor from Exodus is apt. Sometimes the journey presses on, whether or not the participant is ready or willing. And perhaps the system did fail the nominee. Maybe the diocese is not ready yet for an LGBT+ priest; or not ready for too many of them. In some dioceses, the bishop believes he or she is ordaining for the church. In others, the bishop believes he or she is ordaining for his or her diocese. Perhaps trying again is worth the effort, even if it means more months or years, more soul searching, and more heartache.

Or perhaps, it is on to other work in the name of God—work beyond the institution of the Church. As Barbara Cawthorne Crafton writes, "Your life's calling does not need to be ordained beforehand in order to be your life's calling."[1]

There are a host of ways that your calling may be to the role you already play in the world: as a coworker, as a teacher, as a friend, as a mother or father. The work of discernment, if it was to have any value, should have kicked up the dust of possibilities for your life. It should have opened up new ways your talents or gifts may be used to serve God, perhaps through leadership of some kind but perhaps not. The end goal, indeed, the "end" is not ordination—not even for the ordained. The end is God.

In other words, *No* is not always the final answer. And *No* is not an end.

• • •

Not Yet has increasingly become the *No* answer of yore. *Not Yet* means, essentially, that a bishop and/or a Commission on Ministry have not seen or heard enough evidence that the nominee's call is validated. This could be due to any number or reasons, including but not limited to:

- The nominee has only experienced parish ministry in one setting his or her whole life. In this case, the diocese would most likely prescribe a year for the nominee in another church setting entirely. This church, or mission, may be a radical change from the nominee's sponsoring parish setting. If one was raised and sent on through the process from a wealthy suburban parish of some privilege, he or she might then expect to be sent to an urban parish—perhaps one in which English is a secondary language, or one in which there are financial challenges. The point should be clear to the nominee who receives a *Not Yet* in this provision: he or she needs to experience an entirely different facet of the Church.

- The nominee may have simply done poorly in the interviews. Unfortunately, this is sometimes the case. Any number of factors could have led to this. Perhaps he or she could not sleep due to nerves. Maybe he or she was unprepared by the parish in some way, and did not have solid or satisfactory answers to the questions of the Commission.

- The system failed the nominee. For the LGBT+ seeker, this one stings the most. As a minority, a queer nominee should hopefully be prepared (if not, now you are!) that the system will sometimes let you down. There could have been an answer that did not sit well with a member of the Commission, and wouldn't you know it? That person has a lot of clout on the whole governing body and was able to sway others into a negative impression of you. Likewise, maybe you are that nominee that is in a diocese that has only so many "queer" slots to fill; perhaps this is one queer nominee too many. And, sadly, perhaps homophobia comes into play. Even at this level, the Commission on Ministry and those in the episcopate are as human as God is divine. The Church that is laid on Christ as the sure foundation is inevitably going to come up short as a human endeavor that is flawed on many fronts. Sometimes, a diocese simply gets it wrong. And sometimes, as in the *Not Yet* answer, a diocese needs another year to grow into its change.

Though it is not convenient in the slightest, a deferral by a parish, bishop, or Commission on Ministry is usually greeted by nominees as a major learning experience. For many, their time assigned to a year-long project in another parish or mission, or in some specific form of ministry, grants him or her the ability to see greater facets of the priesthood. And indeed, some find avenues of ministry that reveal new possibilities for them, possibilities that do not necessarily *need* to include sacramental ordination. For example, those with wonderful pastoral gifts, but who maybe lack organizational, administrative leadership skills, may be given a chance to learn the ropes of institutional leadership in a large program parish. For the other side of the coin, more pastorally-shy nominees may be assigned work in chaplaincy at a hospital or prison.

Generally speaking, the *Not Yet* pushes back the deadline a bit for the nominee. It is positive because it is not a *No*, even though the possibility of a *No* remains in the picture. But more than likely, the time spent on specific projects assigned by a Commission on Ministry or bishop will satisfy the loose ends on an aspirant's profile. In the same weekend of my postulancy retreat in 2012, two aspirants were granted postulancy following a year serving in a different parish, learning administration.

• • •

I will never forget how frustrated I felt in December of 2000, when Al Gore, my presidential candidate of choice, was stuck in a recount battle. After several weeks of challenges, hanging chads, and finally, a Supreme Court intervention, reality sunk in. Gore had lost, by a mere 537 votes. In the absence of one more recount to be sure, Gore finally had to concede his loss to George W. Bush, who was on track to become the 43rd president of the United States. Of the many critiques of his campaign, Gore had endured an onslaught of criticism about his effectiveness as a speaker to the "common person," devoid of emotion. That changed when he gave his remarkable concession speech to the nation, in which he included this sentence: "While I strongly disagree with the Court's decision, I accept it."

In that moment, Gore showed class and grace, in what must have been one of the most humiliating moments of his life. He easily could have then retired to his private home, hid away and disappeared into obscurity like countless other hopefuls for the Oval Office before him. Instead, Gore transformed his mission in life. He turned to an adjunct tract of politics that focused on the environment and climate change. He became a champion of conservation of our resources, reduction in carbon emissions, and becoming—in a truly Christian way—stewards of our good earth. His documentary *An Inconvenient Truth,* which detailed his analysis of global warming at the hands of humans, won an Oscar in 2006. To both Democrats and moderate Republicans alike, Gore's transformation in his rejection exemplified endurance for the common good.

• • •

What does the queer nominee do with the *No* or the *Not Yet* answer? It happened to be an easier deduction for me to realize my calling would be fulfilled beyond ordained ministry as an active participant or leader in the laity somewhere. For those who are really counting on, or hoping for, ordination as the end, perhaps the task is to endure. As if following Moses in the wilderness, the challenge is to endure this as a test to one's faith and one's certainty of a calling. The discussion early in this book about terming this a "sense of calling" is apt here. One can only sense a calling for ministry, in the Episcopal Church, in the context of a hierarchical system that makes decisions for the greater body. If you strongly disagree with the Court's decision, as Al Gore once put it, you still owe it to the Church to accept it.

Chris Glaser's story in *Uncommon Calling* recalls a time in the greater Church when homosexuality was a disqualifier for ordained ministry. After an extensive discernment process, Glaser was ultimately not approved to be a pastor at the last level of vetting, something akin to the Episcopal Church's diocesan Commissions on Ministry. This underscores the heartbreak for droves of would-be clergy who felt a clear call to ordained ministry, but were not allowed to pursue formal discernment to even test the call. This pain from a time not so long ago, remains present. For his part, Glaser realized it had less to do with his own viability in the calling, but more about the Church's problem with how to integrate its growing complicated body. Glaser describes this moment in our collective LGBT+ faith history that was marred by lack of vision:

> Yes, in the church's inability to integrate lesbian and gay Christians fully into its life, the church lacks integrity. But how can I reject the church for a lack of integrity, when I also struggle to more fully realize this goal? It took years for my sexuality and spirituality to view one another as lovers rather than strangers. I don't expect the church to make the same transformation overnight.[2]

While the Church has moved dramatically into acceptance of queer leaders to postulancy, the reality of this inadequate rendering of a fully integrated body of Christ still exists in the conservative realms of the Church.

For Glaser, this was a sad end of the line by his own choice. In his interpretation of this ending of his formal discernment, Glaser was able to gain a perspective on the ministry of all baptized persons:

> Obviously my ministry did not end with a denial of ordination. The struggle for ordination itself had proven to be ministry. The denial of ordination ironically empowered

my ministry, adding to it the honor that accrues to those who suffer for a compassionate cause and instilling hope in all those who believe in the church's ongoing reformation. While not the perfect outcome, my nonordination enjoyed more integrity than many ordinations.[3]

It is entirely possible that the *No* answer, just like the *Not Yet,* can inspire you to explore different realms of the ever-expanding kingdom of heaven. There will always be a need for the leadership and witness of the laity. But there is also the freedom of the unencumbered leader who can maneuver through the waters of the Church without the vows to a bishop or the duty of the office of priest hung over his or her head. Empowered by the most important vows of all, the baptismal covenant, the nominee can transform his or her potential ministry into one that seeks and serves Christ in all persons.

Nora Gallagher discerned her way out of the priesthood, claiming a *No* in her own right when she realized she is part of William Countryman's "priesthood of all believers"—a priesthood not limited by sacramental leadership but expanded by simply being human. Gallagher describes her newly kindled appreciation for service and outreach as an unencumbered layperson, one who is not bogged down by the administrative and pastoral demands of the literal priesthood:

> I thought of us then as a community of ears, pressed to the earth, to hear the gentle footfalls of the one who is always coming into the world. He offers in place of security the adventure of longing and the fragility of love. He offers a wholeness bought at the cost of suffering. We need to be ready to leap onto that tightrope or else that love will not come. I remembered that in Genesis, God invited Adam and Eve to name the created order, not to subdue it, because naming is our human gift. In this new Eden

we would be invited to name the world again, to name it anew, to name and be named, to listen and to speak, to gather up our gifts and travel toward a new Eden bought at the cost of suffering, an Eden of others.[4]

For Gallagher, and for many who come to the end of discernment with a rejection, there is great liberation to be a fully embodied child of God in the world. It is the kind of radical freedom found in discerning and following where God leads, the kind of hope in vocation that is not deduced to ordination. As Barbara Cawthorne Crafton has pointed out earlier: Each of us has a calling. And the ministry of all baptized persons knows no limits.

Chris Glaser has the final word: "Ordination is not necessary to minister; my ministry had already begun."[5]

Notes

1. Crafton, *Called*, 21.
2. Glaser, *Uncommon Calling*, 207.
3. Ibid., 208.
4. Nora Gallagher, *Practicing Resurrection: A Memoir of Work, Doubt, Discernment, and Moments of Grace* (New York: Alfred A. Knopf, 2003), 184.
5. Glaser, *Uncommon Calling*, 99.

7
Yes

Divided tongues, as of fire, appeared among them, and a tongue rested on each of them. (Acts 2:3)

The sequel to Luke's Gospel is the Acts of the Apostles, a narrative book in the New Testament that details the early beginnings of the Church. In the first chapter of Acts, Jesus ascends to heaven. In the wake of this event, the eleven remaining disciples have to pick up the pieces and start their ministry in his name. They will need a little help, for the teachings of Jesus will not be enough to carry them through their mission. So, as Jesus promised, the "advocate" is sent—the Holy Spirit descending upon the disciples in much the same way as Luke described it descending upon Jesus at his baptism. The scene in Acts 2 is almost comical as the disciples receive the Holy Spirit—in the form of tongues of fire, not a dove this time. They speak in tongues, now suddenly able to communicate in all the languages of the world into which they will spread the gospel. The disciples are empowered in this moment with a sacred blessing that will carry them forward. Their leadership is sanctified, and it is this "Pentecost" moment that is directly evoked in the laying on of hands at ordination.

• • •

When my Commission on Ministry finished deliberating, I was called into another conference room. Two members of the Commission sat with me and my rector, Steve. The door to the room was shut, and I heard the words come out quickly: "It's a yes." The "shepherds," as they would be called, moved quickly onto a listing of expectations and some paperwork that was coming my way. But I heard "yes," and breathed first a sigh of what could only be described as relief. It was relief, because I had an answer, one way or another. The future was now a bit clearer. Then that moment quickly passed, and anxiety washed over me.

• • •

While witnessing another person receive their *No* answer in disbelief at the end of the postulancy retreat weekend was unsettling, I will say the confusion upon receiving the *Yes* answer was almost as startling. For now, the stakes were not so much high as the game was changed.

The *Yes* answer signals a major life change: seminary, whether residential or commuter, is going to be disruptive to one's normal life pattern. A decision must be made. For those who need to maintain an equilibrium of finances, the possibility of a distance-learning experience of seminary may be a reality. This could mean as many as four to six years of schooling in the hours outside of one's primary job. It is a daunting, demanding task, and it is not for the faint of heart.

For those who feel compelled to a classical residential setting for seminary, this means a number of changes. The postulant has to leave his or her main job. The postulant has to move—sometimes across the country, in order to enroll in seminary. The postulant may have to uproot his or her family, find a new part-time or work-study job, and all while studying and preparing for holy orders. And the postulant may have to continually "come out" to friend, family members, and coworkers as a person who is preparing for ordained ministry.

I will never forget the day I scheduled an appointment with the president of the film studio division in which I worked: May 1, 2012. My task was to tell her I was leaving for the priesthood. Being the head of a studio in Hollywood, I realized she may find my change of careers to be unusual, to say the least. I said the words aloud to her, and I will never forget how she threw her head back slowly in her chair absorbing the news. I would like to think it was because I was a tough loss to the company. It likely had more to do with the shock of the rationale.

"Is there anything I can do to keep you?"

That is the greatest response an employer can ever give you when you threaten to leave, indicate you are potentially leaving, or pondering a change. In this instance, in the very short wake of the *Yes* answer that had changed my life and would uproot it for good, I had a number of feelings: I could say, "Yes, please up my pay, give me that raise I have been seeking, how about a new office, and how about an assistant (worth its weight in gold in Hollywood)?" That would be the smart ploy here. But there is that nagging, cloying pull of the Holy Spirit in the wake of the *Yes* answer. The feeling that you are being pulled into a new existence, that is in this case, postulancy, is overwhelming. And it means you have a better handle on what matters and what doesn't matter.

"Nope," I said to my boss. "This is what I am supposed to do."

With that, I said good-bye to my six-figure salary, my rather large office on the 20th Century Fox studio lot in west Los Angeles, my clout as a budding marketer and advertising junior executive, and likely my possible reentry someday if this new path did not work out.

• • •

At the point the nominee receives a *Yes* answer, effectively becoming a postulant, it is off to the proverbial races. What lies ahead in this next stage is a mixture of semi-trauma (a move, possibly involving children and/or pets, and probably involving a long journey of some sort) and glorious joys. For most postulants, the preparation begins for seminary. If it is to be a residential seminary, there will be major transitions. Depending on the seminary chosen in consultation with the bishop, there may be a strain on finances. Even for those lucky enough to secure scholarships or financial aid for graduate school, it is still a major adjustment to becoming a full-time student. For married or partnered couples, a move to a residential seminary usually means both members of the couple are changing jobs or careers.[1] In these cases, not only does the postulant have to adjust to becoming a full-time student, but the spouse or partner has to find work; or perhaps more strenuous, the couple has to cope with one income—or none at all.

This is all separate from the complications of moving to a new city or town and becoming acclimated in a new community. For residential seminaries such as Virginia, General, and Sewanee, for example, there are incredible demands upon the students—and sometimes their families—to participate in the life of the community. But sometimes in addition, there is culture shock. My own Class of 2015 saw the arrival of dozens of families from the deep South who had to navigate living in the Washington, DC, beltway for a change.

If the postulant is to attend seminary part-time, perhaps while maintaining a day job (as many of my colleagues have done), it is still a colossal amount of stress and pressure. Imagine your life suddenly oriented around working forty hours or more a week, studying or writing papers in your free evenings, and attending classes one or more nights or weekends. It becomes an incredibly challenging time, especially for those with families or partners.

At a full-time residential program, the postulant morphs into a round-the-clock graduate student at the start of seminary. If he or she held an office job in the past, they now find themselves consumed with deadlines and reports of a different ilk. They are writing papers, they are attending seminars, and they are reading *a lot*. For many, these are entirely new subjects, things unheard of in their undergraduate experiences: theology, pastoral care, liturgy, and music. For some, this is the first time they are reading the entirety, or close to it, of the Bible.

In the years that follow, the postulant quickly realizes that the euphoria of the *Yes* answer gives way to new anxieties. There are really four major checkpoints along the classic journey of a postulant to holy orders:

1. Clinical Pastoral Education (CPE) internship. In this ten- to twelve-week intensive internship, often taken by postulants in their first summer after beginning seminary, the intern works all day (and sometimes all night) in a hospital or nursing home setting. Usually a postulant in the Episcopal Church must complete his or her CPE unit as a requirement for ordination, and usually the placement is determined in consultation with the sponsoring diocese. CPE is legend. It makes or breaks some postulants. For those who are introverted and perhaps afraid to confront outward processing of emotions, this will be a very challenging internship. For others, there may be consuming feelings of empathy and guilt all wrapped together. For some, being in a hospital setting just may be enough trauma on its own. And the accredited ACPE programs, where most dioceses allow postulants to participate in the CPE programs, usually come with challenging structures: supervisors, group therapy–type discussions, verbatim processing, reflection papers, and lots of analysis. Nevertheless, most postulants come away changed as they enter their subsequent year of seminary. But their experience in CPE is not necessarily behind them.

2. Candidacy. The postulant next has to worry about crossing the threshold into candidacy. A *candidate* is the last stage of the process before becoming an *ordinand*. The candidate is officially preparing for holy orders and is working toward the final checklist of their process before ordination to the transitional or vocational diaconate. This means, you guessed it, another appearance before the Commission on Ministry and potentially the bishop. This tends to happen in the middle of the second year of seminary or the third year, as most Commissions are waiting to see how the postulant fared in CPE as well as their grades in seminary. So in preparation for candidacy interviews, seminarians are usually fretting over their verbatims and reviews from CPE, their grades in their courses, and the second-year evaluations by the faculty and dean's office of their seminary. This is before there is even a trip back to one's diocese to participate in the candidacy retreat weekend. The point of *this* retreat, unlike the postulancy retreat (which is really to suss out the nominee for the task of ministry), is to check in about the postulant's experience preparing for ministry thus far. If all parties see progress, a postulant might usually expect to become a candidate very soon after or immediately.

3. General Ordination Exams (GOEs). For candidates of the Episcopal Church, at least, the next stage following candidacy that causes the greatest amount of anxiety—perhaps greatest of all of these four points—is taking the General Ordination Exams. Affectionately known by their shorthand, the GOEs are the Episcopal Church's version of a lawyer's bar exam.[2] The GOEs have been on the scene for as long as there has been an LGBT+ movement, about fifty years. There is a faint odor in the Church of "I had to do it, so now you have to" among clergy. Candidates are to answer six essay questions over four days in January, taking an allotted three and a half hours to answer each essay question in each canonical area. The system of the GOEs is designed to test the seminary's teaching, in one respect; it also winds up testing the candidate's ability to withstand pressure. But, truthfully, in a medium in which writing is a big deal (sermons, newsletters, and general communication on a pastoral level), the GOEs really test the candidate's ability to synthesize theology and pastoral situations. There are rarely ways around them, although technically the canons stress that a candidate must prove proficiency in the six canonical areas, before he or she may become ordained. That said, like the CPE programs, most if not all dioceses require their candidates to take the GOEs. On one end of the spectrum, there are dioceses (read: bishops) who are not very concerned with the results. There may be a check-in of sorts, or a feigned attempt at a re-explanation of one's answer. But for many bishops, unless the score is zero or one out of six, it is a time to turn the page. For others, though, GOEs are quite serious. Even missing one out of the six exams, that is, receiving a "Not Proficient" may constitute the candidate doing some "make good." This could be in the form of a rewrite, or an e-mail, or phone conversation in which the candidate tries to take a second stab at responding to the question. The good news is that rarely—*rarely*—do candidates fail so miserably that there is a nullification of his or her ordination track.

4. Finding a Job. Almost as soon as the GOEs are completed, and sometimes prior to this, the candidate is on the hunt for a first job. The first position postseminary could be a relatively common one: the *curate* role. A curate is ostensibly a "curer (or carer) of souls," a person set apart for pastoral care in a church setting. In the Episcopal Church, a curate is primarily a first-timer's job, usually a transitional deacon and then a priest, who is given a set of tasks by his or her boss (the rector, in most cases) in a parish. In more rural dioceses, a curate may begin his or her ministry postgraduation as a leader or interim-leader in a small church somewhere. The process of finding these jobs runs the gamut. Staying with those same small parishes, a candidate may have had a job reserved for him or her by a bishop or transition officer (often a canon to the ordinary) as much as three years in advance. On the flip side, some dioceses send their postulants off to seminary with no expectations of finding jobs in their home diocese. In this case, the now-candidate must not only worry about finishing his or her degree but also finding a job. The interview process at this level is competitive; one may be interviewing for jobs for which classmates are also interviewing. The reality of homophobia may rear its ugly head in the most tangible way at this point. Perhaps a church or diocese interviews a handful of seminarians for a job, but cannot afford the political capital of having a queer priest on staff. Or perhaps the allure of a married straight cleric with a spouse and children is too irresistible compared to a gay person. Regardless, this fourth stage can likely be the most treacherous and the most disheartening part of the whole process. It is where the rubber meets the road, really: I am called to holy orders, but will anyone hire me?

And then, of course, there is the very real and likely reality that the postulant who becomes a candidate and meets the needs of the canons and the approval of the Commission on Ministry and bishop will be ordained to the diaconate.[3] This signifies the completion of a race that is really a marathon; for as formal discernment *to the priesthood* completes, the loose thread pulled reveals that discernment will continue. Discernment will permeate the person's life, showing up constantly in small ways, such as making decisions about which readings to pick, or how people should address you, and other innocuous moments. Discernment will also rear back in significant ways: what sort of job you feel called to perform in the church, for example. Are you to be a parish priest, or more of a chaplain? You will need to discern what kind of preacher you are called to be—prophetic social justice or academic, or both (or neither!).

The *Yes* answer is powerfully affirming, but it can also be a bit terrifying. There will be major life changes now, something Nora Gallagher mused about when she started the discernment process:

> If they discerned with me that I was called to the priesthood, it meant a series of leave-takings: I would leave Trinity, the parish I loved, for a year and intern at another church. I would leave my home in Santa Barbara for three years of seminary, and then a job elsewhere in the diocese. I would leave writing, at least for a while, a profession I had practiced for twenty years. And my marriage. What would become of that?[4]

All of these real changes underscore an ontological change happening in the postulant. Now, in the wake of an affirmation of your calling, you are holding a great responsibility. For now, you will be responsible for the pastoral and spiritual lives of your congregants. Your every written or spoken word will be analyzed, misinterpreted, or constantly called back into review. There will be countless times when you feel you have crafted the greatest sermon, and then everyone shuffling out the door of the church will only give you pleasantries. Conversely, there will be times where you cannot sleep because you are not sure you have preached the gospel, only to find out beyond your wildest imagination that the Spirit really did work through you in your words.

There will be small things that actually signify something major about your own personal theology. The decision of when to wear your collar, the sign of the office of the diaconate and priesthood, will be scrutinized by some, not the least of which being your own very self. Are you prepared to don the new apparel and walk through the streets of your town or city with the black shirt and white collar? Many will stop and give you a second look. The homeless will definitely intercept you as you try to head to the bank or grocery store—how much money will you give them, and how will it look to others if you refuse? Or maybe you will choose not to wear your clericals except when tradition demands it.[5]

And all of these are to say nothing about the added layer of pressure and scrutiny concerning the LGBT+ clergy community. If you are partnered or married, you may find yourself pausing when you begin to write your first biography for the parish website. How much information do I want to share about my partner? In fact, this ought to be a universal struggle for anyone, straight or not, although I would wager that a heterosexual priest who decides to speak about his or her partner or children takes less time considering the consequences. Now, if you are single, you may face advantages as well as complications. How will you handle the parishioners who mean well but really want to set you up with someone of the opposite sex at a dinner party? Prior to that, how many invitations to dinner parties will you even accept, period? And how much of your personal life will you intend to share or withhold? Where are your own boundaries, and how will you define them?

For the queer clergyperson, you cannot underscore how much pressure falls upon your shoulders in any one-on-one pastoral encounter. Visibility and corroboration will be key in the sad possible event that your words or counsel could be misconstrued because of the recipient's confusion or conflation of your sexual identity. Even more concerning will be how you interact with the children and youth at your parish, given the public's general confusion that persists about homosexuality and pedophilia. You have to be aware of this scrutiny, whether or not you agree with its merit.

Because of all of these swirling thoughts and pulls of the Spirit, this is the perfect time, in the transition to postulancy, to engage a spiritual director. Like a therapist works on the mind, the spiritual director works on the soul. Priests as well as laypersons are highly encouraged to have spiritual direction for regular work that focuses on the spiritual realm and the journey of calling. In the book *Hearing the Call*, Jonathan Lawson and Gordon Mursell commend spiritual direction this way, "Have a spiritual director or a soul friend, someone they can talk to in complete confidence about the whole of their lives and especially about what God is saying to them."[6]

A spiritual director may help articulate turns in your discernment, and put in context what you are experiencing. Later in life, as work deepens in ministry, a spiritual director may help recalibrate your relationship to the Spirit and what God is working within you. This kind of spiritual companion reminds us that it helps to talk out our thoughts and feelings sometimes in order to perceive them. And perhaps even more importantly, a spiritual director also gives you someone to support you along the way.

The *Yes* answer is a glorious attestation that the sense of call to sacramental leadership was accurate. This is certainly a triumphant moment for the postulant; but it is also okay to be anxious. Things are about to be disrupted, in your life and in your soul. And more will be demanded of you than ever before. For the queer postulant, a whole new set of challenges will present themselves, too. Will I be accepted in a new community? Will I be able to be openly gay and still lead those who do not agree with my sexual orientation? Will I be able to use my gifts properly for ministry?

Adrift seemingly with no bearings even if the path is being distilled to something attainable, it is easy to feel isolated as a queer postulant.

But you will never be alone.

Notes

1. I say "usually" because you would be surprised the number of seminarian spouses I have met in the last five years who work-from-home in fields such as consulting, graphic design, and the like.

2. But considerably less difficult.

3. A vocational deacon will be ordained just this once. A priest is required in the Episcopal Church to be ordained twice: for six months first as a transitional deacon, one who is serving in a preparatory role of servitude in ministry and liturgy. Assuming no other diocesan hurdles or setbacks on the part of the deacon, she or he is then ordained to the Sacred Order of Priests.

4. Gallagher, *Practicing Resurrection*, 18.

5. To demystify that, I can only speak for myself: I wear clericals when I am performing a sacrament, officiating or serving in worship, or representing the Church. I try to avoid wearing clericals when I am doing menial Greg-tasks such as picking up Tide with Bounty or cat food. Mostly because the collar is not very comfortable.

6. Jonathan Lawson and Gordon Mursell, *Hearing the Call: Stories of Young Vocation* (London: Society of Promoting Christian Knowledge, 2014), 42.

CONCLUSION

The truth is rarely pure and never simple.
—Oscar Wilde

In a previous life, long before I was in discernment, back when I had erected structures to blockade my call from God, I was an ad man.[1] Consumed in the world of print media, I helped design and ship newspaper ads on a daily basis for a movie studio. This was a job focused about 20 percent of the time on design, and 80 percent pushing back deadlines to avoid the inevitable. When your life is centered around deadlines, you naturally try to squeeze all the time you can muster. An ad is due Monday at 4 p.m. for *The New York Times*, you say? I am going to need a few more hours. I have until Tuesday at 8 a.m., you say? Good, let me squeeze a few more critics' quotes in before we ship. And you push and you delay, and you drive everyone around you frantic as you dilly-dally. At a certain point, the ad must go or the *Times* will print without your artwork—and then you would really be up the creek. Finally, three hours past due, you have massaged and squeezed text into art and locked the creative, and given the go-ahead to your production team: okay to ship. By the time you make that deadline, what was the cost really? Was it worth it to wait so long, and did you learn anything new in the process? Perhaps the ad never really improved to begin with. And more than likely, you lost a part of your soul in the process as you screamed at designers and ad sales representatives to hold the presses for you. Soon you become accustomed to this—pushing deadlines back. Resisting the inevitable. Late to the call.

Don't do that with God's calling.

For that great segment of the population that feels a spiritual tug at the heart, a pull from God to serve, it is easy to delay listening. The call from God to be a leader is never convenient and rarely simple. For the LGBT+ discerner, things are even more complicated—and more dire. To deny a calling is as fundamentally against the self as denying one's sexual identity. The two are connected. Perhaps the queer person is better equipped to respond to a call from God because he or she has already gone through the process of coming out of the closet—I know that this was true in my case. Or, if he or she is still closeted, I would be shocked if the process of discernment did not have an effect on pushing up that other revelation's particular deadline.

There are stakes now for waiting in responding to God's call. First, there is age. You are not getting any younger, and at a certain point, you may phase out of a fulsome chance to minister. Second, there is the pride; the kind of pride that empowers a queer person to admit his or her sexual identity; a pride matched in the follower of Christ who feels emboldened to be a change agent for the kingdom of heaven. It is pride in the fact that you have answered a calling that "may not be so much a call to 'do' as to 'be.'"[2] Lastly, there is perhaps the greatest stake: the lives of those who are yet to be touched.

When I began writing this book, the world seemed at ease for the LGBT+ community. Politically speaking, we seemed on a trajectory for equality. Hillary Clinton surely would be elected, and the expansion of queer-friendly rights and benefits would continue as they did under

Barack Obama's presidency. And the expanse of progressive values would continue its inevitable trend into the churches across the country: there would be more women, more blacks, more Latinos, more Asians, more queer persons presiding at altars.

Then on November 8, 2016, the story took a dramatic right turn as Donald Trump was elected president of the United States. And since his swearing in, President Trump has, as expected, revoked his claim to support the LGBT+ community. He has made a number of proclamations and executive orders that seemed to infringe on already granted rights to many oppressed peoples in this country. The spread of this fear certainly touched all minorities, causing consternation, frustration, and fear in the LGBT+ community.

For the priesthood, then, the task has changed. For this book, then, the overall goal has changed. I began this on the auspices of LGBT+ clergy becoming the new normal in the Episcopal Church. I write now in 2018 as someone who is afraid of the limits and setbacks that may be placed on us. I worry how this may affect the role of queer clergy, the parishes and missions, and the Church as a whole. Maybe this is no longer the "queer" moment, as it seemed back in 2015 when same-sex marriage became legal. Maybe the LGBT+ leadership in the Church is in danger, and maybe we are marching against the norm and it is not going the "way of history" as is often the defense.

Or, perhaps the gospel of Jesus is still pervasive, no matter the oligarchy in control. Maybe, as the New Testament tells us, the last shall be first and the first shall be last. Perhaps those with queer sexual identities continue to reflect an accurate picture of the body of Christ, a picture of a loving being that crossed boundaries and social constructs by his very nature. The falsehood in the last several years of social acceptance and platitudes in the Church may have simply given us a false view of the world around us, even as we accept ourselves from the inside out. Thomas Bohache puts it, "We are never safe, even when we think we are, even when we have carefully erected an edifice to seal us off from real people with real problems."[3] For as long as there are those struggling with their identity, those who feel weighted down by shame falsely imposed on them by others, and those who seek to serve God despite the queerness of their socially ordered lives, the march goes on for the LGBT+ church leader. No matter the path, be it ordination or something wildly and incredibly more creative and inspiring, the struggle for queer leaders in the church is a struggle worth enduring. And maybe the weight of the struggle of those who have come before us is worth the endurance. For the sake of this truth, bisexual pastor Martha Daniels says:

> Now is the time to be who I am . . . there will always be those who view me as different and will not want my presence, my input, or my gifts . . . the truth is what I am called to speak and to show, in spite of the (possible) consequences.[4]

The *imago dei* still begs the question of us all: did God make me this way? And if the answer is yes, then for what purpose did such a creator create with such ingenuity and unexpected imagination? And why is this life so difficult because of my created being? What am I supposed to do with this life if it is *not* to be tortured for my sexuality? Indeed, perhaps I am to be lifted up *because* of this. The Triune God continues to call those made in his/her image, even if natural attraction, and affection, seem bent on following the road less travelled. God continues to lift up those creatures, with all their complexities and idiosyncrasies and peculiarities. God asks them to put their talents to good use. And God is, to the end, wildly in love with them.

CONCLUSION

The journey of sexual identity is often wrought with pain and tribulation, but it also reaps great joy for the one who endures to the end. The journey of discernment is perhaps less tangibly challenging, but the introspective demand may indeed be just as great. For even in this postmodern world, a world where leaders in our church and beyond can be as diverse as the colors of the rainbow, being gay is as much a true, holy privilege as being called.

Notes

1. Okay . . . I *worked* for ad people.
2. Farnham et al., *Listening Hearts*, 9.
3. Bohache, "Unzipping Church," 13.
4. The Rev. Martha Daniels, "Not Even on the Page: Freeing God from Heterocentrism," in *Sexuality, Religion and the Sacred*, ed. Loraine Hutchins and H. Sharif Williams (London: Routledge, 2014), 13.

FOR FURTHER READING

Discernment

Called by Barbara Cawthorne Crafton
Let Your Life Speak by Parker Palmer
Listening Hearts: Discerning Call in Community by Suzanne G. Farnham, Joseph P. Gill, R. Taylor McLean, and Susan M. Ward
Practicing Resurrection: A Memoir of Work, Doubt, Discernment, and Moments of Grace by Nora Gallagher
Transforming Vocation by Sam Portaro
Uncommon Calling: A Gay Christian's Struggle to Serve the Church by Chris Glaser

Preparation for Seminary or Further Education

An Introduction to Ministry: A Primer for Renewed Life and Leadership in Mainline Protestant Congregations by Ian S. Markham and Oran E. Warder
The New Oxford Study Bible (NRSV) or HarperCollins Study Bible (NRSV)
What to Expect in Seminary? by Virginia S. Cetuk

Formation

Episcopal Etiquette and Ethics by Barney Hawkins
An Introduction to the New Testament by Raymond Brown
Opening the Bible by Roger Ferlo
Opening the Prayer Book by Jeffrey Lee
Understanding Christian Doctrine by Ian S. Markham

The Soul

An Altar in the World by Barbara Brown Taylor
The Heart of Christianity by Marcus Borg
Here If You Need Me by Kate Braestrup
Jesus Freak by Sara Miles
Living on the Border of the Holy by L. William Countryman
A Priest Forever by Carter Heyward
Searching for Sunday: Loving, Leaving and Finding Church by Rachel Held Evans
Where God Hides Holiness: Thoughts on Grief, Joy and the Search for Fabulous Heels by Laurie M. Brock and Mary E. Koppel
The Wounded Healer by Henri Nouwen

Queer Theology & LGBT+ Topics

Are You Running With Me, Jesus? by Malcolm Boyd
God and the Gay Christian by Matthew Vines
In the Eye of the Storm: Swept to the Center of God by Gene Robinson
The Queer Bible Commentary, edited by Deryn Guest, Robert E. Goss, Mona West & Thomas Bohache
Queering Christianity by Robert Everett Shore-Goss and Thomas Bohache
Radical Love: Introduction to Queer Theology by Patrick S. Cheng

ACKNOWLEDGMENTS

Just as the process of discernment is collaborative in the greatest sense, a book such as this exists only through the participation and inspiration of so many important people. I would like to single out just a few.

Everyone at Church Publishing is gambling on this first-time author, and for that, they should be commended (or possibly committed). Davis Perkins was the editor who greenlit the project, and showed the initial support from the proposal stage. After his retirement, Nancy Bryan took control of the book and was incredibly supportive throughout its composition. Her initial conversation with me, advising me to speak with my own voice, was the spark that really ignited my passion to commence writing. I am so grateful to Amy Wagner and Ryan Masteller for their editing and proofing work on this book, as well.

The parish of St. Paul's Episcopal Church, in Alexandria, Virginia, served as my pastoral home and workplace while this book was conceived and written. I am forever grateful to the staff, clergy, and parishioners who demonstrated unbelievable grace with me as I snuck in hours of writing. That they did not find me too haggard, tired, or confused each day is stunning. Most of all, this would not have been possible without the guidance and support of the rector of St. Paul's, and my dear friend, Oran Warder.

There are names mentioned in this book that are worth repeating, because of their impact on me and countless others. Maryetta Anschutz, Gabriel Ferrer, and Mary Haddad, in particular, all may not have realized their importance in my life at the time—but I hope they do now. Mary Glasspool continues to be an inspiration to me, and I was honored when she agreed to write the foreword and read the manuscript. This touches off the list of contributing readers, who proofread and suggested thematic changes large and small: Crystal Hardin, Barney Hawkins, Ross Kane, Lisa Kimball, and Barbara Warder. It was incredibly helpful to have others to bounce ideas off of, especially Dr. Tyger Latham, who gave a critical eye to the psychological, health, and medical research in the book; Jacob Pierce, my colleague from seminary, who shared his own story and thoughts with me at several points during research; and my informal group of clergy peers and close seminary friends—Will Compton, Chris Hamby, Chandler Irwin, Mary Alice Matheson, and Jennifer Southall—listened to me whine about deadlines, work, fears, hopes, and everything in between. All of these people cheered me on, and corrected me when needed along the way.

However, this book would simply not have happened without Ian Markham. As my seminary dean and mentor on other projects, he has been a meaningful leader and guide. As one of the wittiest and most relatable theologians of the Church, he is an inspiration to many, many more. He shaped the proposal in its infancy, pushed me out on stage to be the sole author, and endorsed me to the publisher. His style, humor, insightfulness, and passion are all imprinted on me and throughout this book. I am forever grateful.

Finally, I acknowledge my husband, Andrew Rutledge, who eleven years on is still the most amazing person I have ever known. His love and support, even in this craziest of all ventures, is still remarkable to me. I just do not deserve him.

ACKNOWLEDGMENTS

This book is dedicated to the resilient ones in the Church, to those LGBT+ persons who long ago tried to sort out their calling but were rejected by the Church at a time when the institution was not yet ready. Their loss is still felt by the queer leaders like me who are here because of their witness. It is dedicated to the persons who are struggling to figure out their sexuality and their identity, no matter where they fall on a spectrum from gay to straight. And it is dedicated to all of us who still seek to find where God wants us to go, and to uncover who God created us to be.

www.ingramcontent.com/pod-product-compliance
Ingram Content Group UK Ltd.
Pitfield, Milton Keynes, MK11 3LW, UK
UKHW021841140426
5217IPUK00022B/1546